About the Author

Jon J. Conrad has directed or produced over 1,000 television commercials for many major companies. He has worked with, among others, Mahalia Jackson, Bess Myerson, Charlie Ruggles, Vincent Price, Betty Furness, and Mike Wallace. He is on the Chicago coordinating council of the Directors Guild of America and a member of the National Academy of Television Arts and Sciences.

THE

TV
COMMERCIAL
How It Is Made

THE

COMMERCIAL
How It Is Made

Jon J. Conrad

 VAN NOSTRAND REINHOLD COMPANY
New York Cincinnati Toronto London Melbourne

Printed in the United States of America
Designed by Rose Della Vasquez

Published by Van Nostrand Reinhold Company Inc.
135 West 50th Street
New York, New York 10020

Fleet Publishers
1410 Birchmount Road
Scarborough, Ontario M1P 2E7, Canada

Van Nostrand Reinhold Australia Pty. Ltd.
480 Latrobe Street
Melbourne, Victoria 3000, Australia

Van Nostrand Reinhold Company Limited
Molly Millars Lane
Wokingham, Berkshire, RG11 2PY England

16 15 14 13 12 11 10 9 8 7 6 5 4 3 2 1

Library of Congress Cataloging in Publication Data

Conrad, Jon J., 1920-
The TV commercial.
   Includes index.
   1. Television advertising. I. Title. II. Title:
Television commercial.
HF6146.T42C63 1983   659.14′3   82-16056
ISBN 0-442-21866-4
ISBN 0-442-21867-2 (pbk.)

Acknowledgments

Many associates helped me in preparing this book. I am particularly indebted to Professor Jack Sissors of Northwestern University for suggesting it; Tom Tucker for helping me organize it; Andy Costikyan for moral support, illustrations, and reference material; and Victor Duncan for help in obtaining equipment illustrations.

CONTENTS

PREFACE
A Short History of Broadcast Advertising

It seems as though I have always been in the picture business. My father was a pen-and-ink artist, and my mother colored Christmas cards for her friends in the entertainment profession during the 1930s. My older brother was a layout artist and executive with a commercial art studio.

I started my working days as a production man in an advertising agency but left for a stint in the air force as a photographer and laboratory chief. After my discharge, I worked as a darkroom technician and still photographer for a company that made catalogs and slide films. As the company grew I graduated into industrial motion pictures, first as a cameraman and later as a director. It was in this capacity that Dan Ryan, the radio director at Taitham-Laird Advertising Agency in Chicago, came to me in the infancy of television and said, "You're a motion-picture man and I write radio copy. I'll write radio commercials and you make motion pictures to go along with them and we'll make television commercials."

Thus began my thirty-year career directing and producing telvision com-

mercials. From the experience of more than one thousand commercials comes this book about how television commercials are made. This is a nuts-and-bolts text for students of broadcast advertising; whether they are interested in creative work or in commercial production, the information in this book explains some of the mysteries.

Before discussing television, I turn briefly back to the golden era of radio. As the Dan Ryan story suggests, television commercials were originally extensions of radio commercials; it is therefore important to understand yesterday in order to deal with today and prepare for the electronic horizons of tomorrow.

In the mid-1930s and early 1940s, radio was king. Almost every broadcast was a live performance. Programs and commercials were made in a studio with actors (called voice actors, since they were only heard) grouped around microphones and a sound-effects man and his paraphernalia in a corner ready to help the audience visualize the action. Soap operas, the housewife-oriented dramas sponsored by large soap manufacturers, filled the daytime hours; evening hours were taken up with dramatic, comedy, or variety shows. On some of the dramatic shows, for both physical and economic reasons, actors doubled and tripled voices.

The advertising agencies produced not only the radio commercials but the programs themselves, which regularly attracted audiences of millions. In some cases the agency contracted programs to independent producers. Whichever the case, the agencies bought time from the radio stations or networks; this permitted them to sponsor a complete program or any part of it, as they desired. It also gave the advertising agency the largest share of the sponsor's money. Programs produced by the networks or local stations were usually "sustaining," meaning unsponsored. This pattern was not to be repeated in the television industry.

Radio commercials in those days were usually live and performed by an announcer (generally the program host) or by regulars and guests on the program. Because the advertising agency produced both the programs and the commercials, this posed no problem. Each program usually had only one sponsor. On the Lux Radio Theater, which featured movie stars, a condition of employment was an on-the-air endorsement of the product.

Until the early 1940s, the radio industry did not have the technology to permit programs to be recorded and broadcast with live fidelity. Then vinyl discs were developed, and programs and commercials could be recorded with live quality. These electrical transcriptions became the standard method of radio broadcasting.

Many advertisers had their own studios that were used for rehearsals, commercials, and even program recording; although broadcast was always made by the station, which had the proper equipment and licenses for the air frequency. Musical commercials became stylish. Jingles were recorded by the big bands of the era; the familiar themes of Pepsodent toothpaste, Lucky Strike cigarettes, and other popular products of the day are still remembered and have become standards of their kind.

The production of radio commercials had a kind of casualness that was to be denied television commercials. Some of this was inherently possible in a sound-only medium, in which a voice actor such as Paul Barnes in "Calling All Detectives" averaged eight to ten characters in one show. In television, the loss of a major performer can doom a series; in radio, when Hal Peary of "The Great Gildersleeve" retired, the Gildersleeve character continued undaunted from the vocal cords of another regular on the show, Will Waterman. Commercials could be changed at any point in production simply by a rewrite and reread. Also, the lack of broadcast-quality transcriptions hindered the rigorous committee review that is now common in advertising agencies.

In 1946 a major advance in audio recording was achieved which also benefited television: a thin iron-oxide coating placed on acetate tape magnetically recorded electrical impulses originated by sound. This tape, which could be edited with a razor blade, produced superb quality sound. The same basic material, videotape, is used for television recording.

Radio continued as a viable national broadcast medium with good advertising support until the late 1950s, when it gradually changed into the local, low-cost-advertising medium of today.

Nineteen forty-eight is the year generally credited with the beginning of practical commercial television. In 1950, as black-and-white television sets came on the market at a price the public could afford, it was evident that this industry had tremendous growth potential. The federal government had broken up the National Broadcasting Company's (NBC) original Red and Blue radio networks into the American Broadcasting Company (ABC) and NBC, and these radio networks moved into television. The only other national radio broadcasting company, Columbia Broadcasting System (CBS), became the third television network. By law, these networks can own only five television stations in the United States. These are referred to as ''O and O (owned and operated) stations'' and are usually located in such major markets as New York, Los Angeles, and Chicago. The networks also have agreements with other stations all over the nation; these stations, called affiliates, split sponsors' commercial payments with the network. Many local stations are not happy with their proportion of this split.

In the early television days, the main unions involved in television broad-. casting were the American Federation of Radio and Television Artists (AF-TRA), the Radio and Television Directors Guild (RTDG), the International Alliance of Theatrical and Stage Employees (IATSE), the International Brotherhood of Electrical Workers (IBEW), and the American Federation of Musicians (AF of M).

National television programs were all broadcast live with a delayed-broadcast capability, using a motion picture called a kinescope made by photographing the television screen. Commercials were either live or on film. Some of the very early black-and-white programs were kinescoped, and these films are the only record available. Live and film were the early stations' only capabilities.

Most stations installed a film-projection system before they purchased TV cameras. This system is called a film chain because it interlocks with the broadcast equipment. The typical TV-station film chain could show 3¼-by-4¼-inch cards on a balopticon projector, 2-by-2-inch slides, 16-mm motion pictures, and sometimes 35-mm slide films. In New York, Los Angeles, and Chicago, 35-mm motion-picture projection was also available and, until 1975, specifications for network commercials called for 35-mm prints with a 16-mm backup print.

Most early television programs were motion pictures or multicamera live presentations produced by the stations or networks and sold to advertisers. Commercials were frequent and, although many large companies were sole sponsors of complete shows— Philco Playhouse, Texaco Variety Hour, Westinghouse Theater, Kraft

Theater—local stations could drop in their commercials during the station-identification breaks. Following the lead of radio, most early television commercials were live, broadcast at the same time that they were performed. As is common to all live commercials, mistakes can be made, and there were some beauties. A classic was the Westinghouse vacuum-cleaner commercial that was demonstrated live by Betty Furness for a national audience. After unsuccessfully attempting to assemble and start it, she finally pushed it away and started to laugh. At the local level there were many instances of cameras staying on performers as they spat out liquids they had originally consumed with smiles. The lighting of the filtered end of cigarettes was also extremely common.

The extra expense of filming commercials became justified, and today all commercials are filmed or taped, not only to eliminate mistakes but to enable review and approval. The only exceptions are those spots that use live performance to reinforce a concept. Two recent campaigns by the J. Walter Thompson Advertising Agency used live demonstrations: The Schlitz Super Bowl interviews with beer drinkers and the Sears lawn-mower commercials that document the number of times the machine can be started on the first pull. Both campaigns were extremely successful.

The typical production price for filmed commercials in the 1950s was $5,000 for one minute and $3,000 for twenty seconds. National programming was almost exclusively produced and controlled by the networks and originated in New York, Chicago, or Los Angeles.

Color television first became a factor in broadcasting in 1955; the following year it was estimated that 2 percent of the television sets in use were color. By 1975 the figure had topped 75 percent. Videotape replaced kinescopes for black-and-white television recording; both pictures and sound were recorded on two-inch magnetic tape. In a very short period of time, two-inch magnetic tape was adapted to color. Because of two-inch color-videotape recordings, it was possible to semiautomate stations by the late 1960s. Semiautomation meant that engineering and administration crews could be kept at a minimum, particularly on night shifts, and cassettes (containers) of commercials—or programs—would automatically drop into their proper time slot. The Radio and Television Directors Guild merged with the Directors' Guild of America (DGA) in 1960. This further integrated the film industry and the television industry.

As radio has its AM and FM, so television has its VHF (very high frequency) and UHF (ultra high frequency). VHF stations are usually network-dominated, and the networks controlled television. UHF was an important addition; in a market like Chicago, air time for a thirty-second commercial might cost $500 on a VHF station and $200 on a UHF station.

In the 1970s, computers, solid-state circuitry, and the microcircuit or integrated circuit arrived. Unwieldy studio cameras were miniaturized, and the hand-held electronic news gathering (ENG) camera took its place in the industry. By 1978 news shows used small battery-powered ENG cameras with ¾-inch recorders and were able to tape or live-broadcast a program many miles away from the station. Film cameras almost disappeared from local and network news as the electronic cameras took their place. With the improvement of lenses and pickup tubes, the light levels needed for video cameras were greatly reduced, permitting location shooting with a minimum of lights; existing lights were sometimes sufficient.

A new union, the National Association of Broadcast Employees and Technicians (NABET), was created to represent all the technicians in the broadcast field. The IBEW and IATSE still represent some technical workers in television broadcasting, but their long-standing power in the entertainment field is challenged by NABET.

No one knows what lies ahead in an industry about to welcome fiber optics, digital recording, video discs, ¼-inch videotape recorders and players, high-definition television, even three-dimension broadcasting. Motion pictures are looking at cable TV and the networks are worrying about their future. These are topics of much speculation. However, there is one point on which everyone agrees: no matter what direction television takes, commercials will always be part of it.

CHAPTER

THE ADVERTISING AGENCY

Most television commercials are created, produced, and placed on the air by an advertising agency. The agency is hired by a company to advertise and promote the sale of its product or services. Magazines, radio, newspapers, and television—the advertising media—sell their space or time to advertising agencies at a 15 percent discount; the agency bills its client, the advertiser, at the full price. In addition, all production charges and internal direct costs on each project are billed to the client at cost plus a 15 percent markup. These 15 percents should permit the advertising agency to show a profit.

STAFF

No matter what type of advertising is produced, a medium-sized agency usually consists of the following departments, each with its own director:

1. Management
2. Account service
3. Creative writers and art directors
4. Production
5. Media
6. Research and testing
7. Traffic

Whether an advertising agency has each of these departments or not, all the functions must be performed. If the advertising agency is heavily involved in broadcast, all these departments will have television and radio specialists. The creative and production departments will have writers and storyboard artists who specialize in television commercials, and the production department will have television producers and a television business manager. As each department is examined, our main interest will be its contribution to television production.

Management

An advertising agency must be well managed. The management department is responsible for cash flow, credit, expenditures, and costs billable and unbillable. Above all, it is management's responsibility to make sure the agency makes a profit. This means that overhead must be controlled, a difficult achievement in broadcast production. Many agencies have been forced to set up separate broadcast business departments. Contracts, talent payments, partial billings, additional charges that are billable, schedules, and credit are all production details that relate to broadcast management.

Account Service

The relationship between the client and the advertising agency is extremely important; usually this is handled by account-service people. In some agencies the owner or creative director controls accounts and is the agency account supervisor. As the size of the agency increases or as service needs increase, additional account people are added. With very big advertisers, each account service executive might have special expertise and be responsible for details in one specific area.

Sometimes the client (the company with the product or service to sell) and an agency account-service person get involved with the actual production of the commercial. Although this is somewhat unusual, very large advertisers such as Procter & Gamble and Sears have television commercial producers in their own advertising departments who are assigned to each production as the advisor to agency production. The agency's account executive usually has a prime responsibility for all presentations to the agency client, from original sales plan to completed commercial. Although the extent of an account person's duty varies from agency to agency, the standard one is to keep the client happy.

Creative

These are the planners, the people with ideas. This group makes what an advertising agency sells: they create the scripts and storyboards for production. The size of the agency, the type of accounts, and the number of accounts determine the organization of the planning staff. Most large agency heads were once creative directors. In the small agencies the owner or account supervisor may also function as the creative director, and even do the actual writing. At the other extreme, large agencies have creative directors, associate creative directors, group creative directors, writers, art directors, and, above them all, a creative review group.

The size of the creative department does not change the requirements of a good television commercial. In the usual thirty seconds of air time, the sales message must be properly presented. The ad must be prepared in a manner that will motivate the viewer not only to notice the commercial, but also to remember the product and purchase it at a later date. This is a tremendous challenge. It is particularly difficult because the concept and writing are continuously being reviewed by individuals and committees to make sure they are being handled in accordance with the research, agreed-upon product strategy, and network and legal demands.

Most creative results grow out of the teamwork between writer and art director. This combination originated with print advertising; but because television is also a words-and-picture medium, this team is a practical association for broadcast advertising.

Production

Production people supervise the making of the ads. The television producer is the most prominent member of this group, which also includes business people and many production assistants. There is a considerable amount of department overlap in TV-commercial production, but creative is one of the most visible. It is becoming quite common for writer/producers and art director/producers to function as agency production supervisors. The prime concerns of production are quality, schedule, and cost.

Media

The media department purchases space and time. It is constantly aware of available prime-time buys and the audience demographics. Much wheeling and dealing is done to make the best possible use of the money spent. In fact, many rush commercial productions are needed because of bargain-time buys that allow only a brief lead time in which to prepare the ad.

Time can be purchased from networks or local stations through representatives in most major markets. This time is purchased in lengths of ten seconds, thirty seconds, one minute, and sometimes two minutes or longer on specials; thirty seconds seems to be the most popular amount.

Research and Testing

An intelligent planning approach needs research. Not all agencies have their own research departments, but a number of independent research companies are available as suppliers. Many completed commercials are tested before they are committed to large time buys. Test commercials are a significant part of commercial production; of the more than one thousand commercials I have directed, at least 25 percent were some type of test commercial.

Many commercials are produced for test markets only. Research indicates that two-thirds of the new products tested never get past the test market.

Traffic

Although traffic people are not deeply involved in production, they are essential to good broadcasting. This department is responsible for the procurement and delivery of the finished slides, art, copy, films, and videotapes to the stations. A traffic department can work through a print-distribution company if time and volume permit; a print-distribution company orders quantity film prints or tape dubbings, inspects them, ships them to stations, and stores extras and returned material. On many occasions, traffic must deal directly with the production company to meet schedules. Traffic work may not be extremely glamorous but it is extremely important.

A traffic department handles everything from a $10 slide for a $50 time buy to a $200,000 commercial for a $1 million time buy. Most television commercials fall between these two extremes.

THE AGENCY AND ITS ACCOUNTS

The size of an advertising agency and the type of accounts serviced modify the simple organization described above. All agencies are interested in increasing their billings, but a "sales manager" title is extremely rare; however, the title of "new business manager" is very common. A new business executive has the responsibility of adding new accounts to the agency and usually does this by advertising, prospecting, presenting, and closing. Personal and social ties are an important part of acquiring new business, but the most important factor is previously successful campaigns. Some very successful advertising agencies do not actively solicit new accounts but only accept invitations to make presentations.

Many large advertising agencies simplify their operation by splitting account services, creative, and production into separate account groups. These groups function within the agency as separate agencies handling a small group of accounts, but with the added benefit of using the services of the overall organization when necessary. International and branch offices also work as independent units communicating with the home office when necessary.

When Leo Burnett first started the agency that bears his name, he felt that no advertising agency could give good service to more than a dozen accounts. Since his death, the Leo Burnett Company has become one of the world's largest, but each group and separate office abides by his original conviction.

The 15 percent discount permitted to agencies when they purchase air time on television networks can result in tremendous profits when million-dollar time buys are made. When thirty seconds of commercial time on the Super Bowl costs more than a quarter of a million dollars, the potential is obvious. The large amounts of money involved have created changes in some agency-client relationships. Many large companies such as Quaker Oats and Santa Fe Industries have formed their own advertising agencies and place their own commercials. These so-called captive agencies can be full service, with a complete agency organization, or can exist only to purchase media time at a discount and must subcontract creative, production and traffic work. If time purchases do not generate enough income to make handling an account profitable for an independent advertising agency, an additional fee is sometimes paid by the client.

Advertising agencies find it very difficult to make a profit on the actual production of television commercials. Only those individuals who work on the specific jobs are billable to a client, and although outside production costs are marked up 15 percent there are always questions at the end of production about billable items. I once directed a "dry" commercial for an agency that would not approve a weather day in the budget. When the sunny skies on the tennis court turned to rain, I waited as long as possible and then completed the spot in the rain. When the agency saw the soaking wet commercial, we were paid to reshoot and never had any more prob-alems about allowances for weather days with that agency. If I had not completed the shoot in the rain, there would have been considerable discus-sion about extra billing.

STEPS IN THE CREATIVE PROCESS

The idea or concept of each com-mercial is of major importance. Every agency has a different method of arriv-ing at the premise for a commercial. Since this book is mainly concerned with the production of television com-mercials, the amount of time and tal-ent that is expended by advertising agencies in designing an advertising campaign can only be touched upon. The following could very well be the procedure in a fairly large agency that has decided on television advertising as the best medium for a specific product.

Planning

The first step in planning is a meet-ing of the persons who the agency feels should be involved and could contribute to the project. This group might include account people, the cre-ative director and some writers, an art director, research, a media person, and possibly a TV business manager. After all have been informed of the goals, problems, and overall advertis-ing direction, they are asked to come up with the ideas in their specialty at a second meeting; at this meeting, ideas are presented and dissected. A num-ber of approaches by the creative de-partment are presented, and after dis-cussion the ones to be scripted and

storyboarded are agreed upon. More internal meetings follow before the presentation to the client. In large agencies these meetings could involve a dozen persons; in a small agency two might do the same job. The crea-tive group has many ongoing meet-ings and discussions before they fin-ish.

Scripts

A writer is assigned to submit a script with pictures (video) and sound track (audio) specified in detail. TV-commercial scripts have a somewhat standard form (Figure 1-1). A voice-over (off-screen) audio for a one-min-ute commercial generally has between 100 and 120 words. As with any writ-ing, this script is reviewed and edited many times before it is approved for presentation to the client.

A knowledgeable TV-commercial writer should have a general under-standing of production costs; a good script can be dumped if production costs are out of line. The production department is able to estimate costs and production time if there is any question in the writer's mind. There is no formula for a good script, but the familiar five rules apply:

1. Make it clear
2. Make it complete
3. Make it important
4. Make it personal
5. Make it demanding

Small agencies are sometimes very successful in creating good commer-cials using free-lance writers and art directors. When the script has been approved by the proper supervisors (usually creative director and account manager), it is given to an art director for storyboard preparation.

Storyboards

To prepare a storyboard, the artist illustrates a key frame from each scene

---

RADIO/TELEVISION

Client: Sears, Roebuck and Co.	*Date:* October 12
Product: Microwave	*Revision:* AS PRODUCED
P.O. 1F 1685	*Specifications:* December Microwave SRHR 1332

		VIDEO	AUDIO
1			
2		OPEN ON GIFT PACKAGE ANIMATION.	FRED HOLLIDAY: Opening now at Sears,
3			a Christmas of red ribbon
4		WIPE TO MS FRED AND MICROWAVE.	values. Save a hundred dollars on
5		SUPERS: SAVE $100 NOW ONLY $499.95	Sears best Kenmore microwave oven.
6		AVAILABLE IN MOST SEARS RETAIL STORES	With the eighty-recipe memory,
7		MINIMUM SAVINGS NATIONALLY	
8			
9		CUT TO ECU MICROWAVE CONTROL PANEL.	just pick a recipe number
10		CUT TO WS FRED, MICROWAVE AND TABLE FULL OF FOOD.	and you can cook any of these dishes!
11			
12		CUT TO CU MICROWAVE. DOOR OPENS REVEALING FOOD INSIDE.	Or cook a whole meal, three dishes ready to serve at one time.
13		SUPER: ALL FOOD SHOWN HAS BEEN COOKED IN THIS	
14		MODEL MICROWAVE	
15		CUT TO MS FRED AND MICROWAVE. ZOOM IN ON	Just one touch of new Speed Keys
16		CONTROL PANEL.	
17		CUT TO CU OF COOKED ROAST BEEF WITH MORTICE	sets temperatures for many recipes
18		OF ECU OF CONTROL PANEL.	
19		CUT TO CU OF CAKE WITH MORTICE OF ECU OF CONTROL	and one touch power settings, too.
20		PANEL.	
21		CUT TO MS OF FRED AND MICROWAVE.	Save a hundred dollars, now!
22		SUPERS: SALE ENDS DECEMBER 24TH	
23		PRICE AND DATE MAY VARY IN ALASKA AND HAWAII	
24			
25			

Figure 1-1. Sample script format for a national commercial.

in the script (Figure 1-2). These frames are then assembled in order with lines of copy below each picture. When completely assembled, this group of drawings and words is called a presentation storyboard. Many times this large storyboard is reduced in size and duplicated for ease in handling and distribution. Small storyboards vary in format; all of them usually include scene description, sound specifications, and scene illustrations. There are no hard-and-fast rules in the preparation of storyboards. Their function is to communicate a sense of the commercial.

Many directors of television commercials prefer working from a rough storyboard. My personal preference is to work from a script and refer to the storyboard to see what was presented to the client. I have yet to take a finished commercial and compare it to the original storyboard. To my way of thinking, even if a bad commercial looks just like the storyboard, it is still a bad commercial.

CLIENT PRESENTATIONS

Presenting the finished scripts and storyboards to a client for production approval is a specialized part of agency procedure. There are a number of ways that this presentation can be made; here are a few that I think are typical.

Standard

Scripts and reduced black-and-white duplicates of the color presentation storyboards are handed out to everyone involved in the presentation. This group usually consists of some people including the advertising manager, representing the client, and a group from the advertising agency that usually includes the account supervisor, creative director, management representative, and anyone else required. The large color presentation storyboard is placed in a visible, well-lit area. The presenter reads from the script while describing the screen action. This is the most common presentation, and it is very dependent on the presenter's skill.

Audio-Visual Slide Presentation

This type of presentation needs one or two slide projectors, an audio tape player, and a projection screen. The storyboard is photographed one frame at a time on two-by-two-inch slides. The sound track is recorded, sometimes by a professional announcer. The slides are then projected accompanied by the recording. The slides can be manually changed by referring to the script, but if two projectors are available with an interlocked mechanism that permits one projector's image to dissolve into the other's, the presentation is even more effective. Slide equipment with the dissolving mechanism is standard equipment in many agency projection rooms (Figure 1-3).

Film Animatic Presentation

This is a 16-mm sound film made of each scene in the original color storyboard. It is usually photographed on an animation stand with as much movement incorporated into the shooting as the board permits; this film can give a good approximation of the

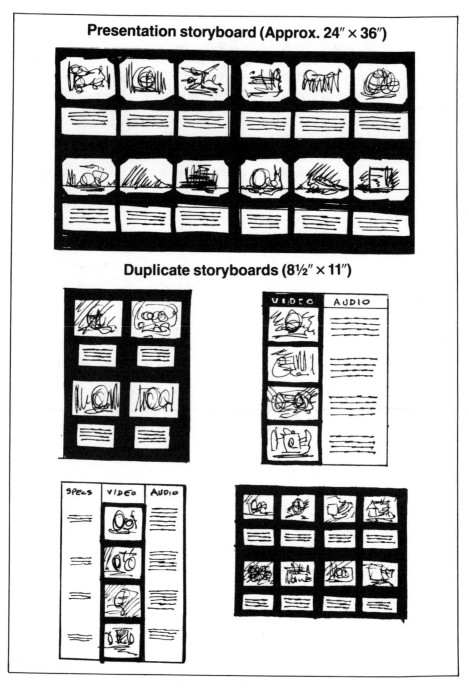

Figure 1-2. Typical storyboard formats.

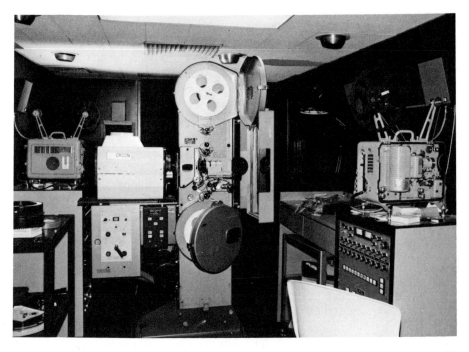

Figure 1-3. An advertising-agency projection room with two 16-mm projectors and an interlock 35-mm projector.

commercial. The sound tracks should be of fairly professional quality for this type of presentation. Many companies supply film animatics for meetings and simple testing.

The word *animatic* comes from the name of a 1950 single-frame projector that was used to present proposed commercials or theatrical playlets. Its frame-change action was extremely fast and it was possible to simulate optical effects and a semblance of movement. It was hand-cued to a presenter or prerecorded sound recording. The name is now used to describe any inexpensive semimotion production used for presentation, usually with sound, on film or tape.

Videotape Animatic Presentation

A videotape animatic can also be produced, and the great number of 3/4-inch videotape players owned by advertising agencies and industry has made an excellent method of presentation. An agency that has a recorder/player and small camera can produce a videotape animatic if editing facilities are available. Videotape-finishing companies are usually able to produce these tapes inexpensively. Animatic videotapes are sometimes suitable for simple testing purposes.

Motion-Picture Presentation

For big-budget productions and major time buys when the total expenditure could be millions of dollars, live photography, original music, professional voices, and anything else that the budget can stand are incorporated in presentation commercials. They are usually photographed on 16-mm film and sometimes produced in-house (by the agency's own staff). Clients occasionally finance this type of commercial to reinforce their own judgment and to have something available for immediate testing.

TESTING

The testing of television commercials is an industry within an industry. When large amounts of money are involved, the advertiser and advertising agency are particularly concerned about the commercial's effectiveness. There are varying opinions about testing. Leo Burnett built his advertising agency without a very high regard for research and testing. On the other hand, David Ogilvy of Ogilvy and Mather has said in *Confessions of an Advertising Man* (Atheneum Press), 1980 that testing and research are very important elements of good advertising.

Testing companies go in and out of business with great frequency, but some have been around for many years and appear to be successful. Many ad agencies have their own testing services. These in-house units show commercials to a group of employees in the office, or show the commercials in projection trailers to shoppers at shopping centers. Independent testing companies also use the shopping-center approach with post-viewing questionnaires. Another method of testing is theatrical screen-ing of TV pilot shows with commercials in place.

There are many techniques involved in measuring audience reaction to these commercials. Test markets are effective for testing commercials and products. This is how they work: a controllable and semiisolated market such as Green Bay, Wisconsin, is selected. After local stores are well stocked with the product, an advertising campaign is mounted. Different commercials might be used, newspaper ad support might be tried, and any other variation of merchandising could be utilized. The final sales records indicate the effectiveness of the specific advertising. Test-market commercials are usually well-produced commercials. If a test product succeeds or if the commercials indicate a good buyer response, the identical commercial can be broadcast nationally.

Testing is usually a requirement specified by clients; the amount of money spent in television advertising seems to warrant this kind of insurance.

The major complaint of many people in production, particularly directors and cameramen, is that an inexpensive spot that has tested successfully puts severe restrictions on the finished commercials. The close supervision of the agency makes it very difficult to maintain the freshness and creative touches that helped make the test commercial successful. This was the case with some inexpensive black-and-white test commercials that I directed for Red Kettle soups. We shot them on location in five hours on

December 24. The five-year-old actor had a runny nose and was the nephew of the agency producer. We had no legal limits and a very loose script. The test scores were great, so the agency went "first class" for the finished commercial. It was cast in Hollywood because the boy with the runny nose could not take time off from school. A large set was constructed on a sound stage and a top director was chosen for the job. There was a lot of supervision and the best agency producer got the assignment. The finished job was beautiful with great color. The little boy had red hair and freckles—real Americana! It all should have worked out beautifully, but it didn't come anywhere close to the test commercial's score. No one could figure out why, and the product is no longer on the grocery shelves.

The goal of the presentation is client approval of the proposed advertising campaign with authorization to proceed. The research, testing, and client discussions that precede the presentation usually result in this approval, with comments and suggestions. Complete rejection probably indicates that the account is in trouble. There are some occasions, such as changes in company policy or management, when the agency must go back to the drawing boards and come up with a new approach. When the advertising campaign is approved, the commercials involved are reviewed and analyzed before production begins.

CHAPTER

TYPES OF COMMERCIALS

Most TV-commercial writers must feel that they are always creating a commercial that has never been done before. Without this viewpoint it would be very difficult to enjoy working in the profession. Although the primary goal of any television commercial is to motivate buying, a secondary objective seems to be winning awards. There are many awards; the Clio, given by the National Television Commercials Festival, is one of the most prestigious awards in this country, and the Cannes Film Festival Lion is a highly prized international award (Figures 2-1 and 2-2). One unfortunate aspect of these awards is that a prize-winning commercial is not always a successful one. One of the most widely known examples is the "spicy meatball" Alka Seltzer commercial. Although the big award winner that year, its advertising agency lost the account because sales were disappointing. There have been so many examples of this problem that some agencies will not permit their commercials to be entered in any competitions.

What makes a successful commercial? There is no simple answer to this question. Humor seems to be an excellent approach for winning awards and, in spite of the above example, is sometimes very effective in increasing sales. Federal Express credits its humorous commercials for a great deal of its success. Unfortunately, its competition appears to by copying its production technique, a fairly common occurrence that adversely affects all commercials.

The targeted audience must also be considered in the writing, production, and time buys. Saturday morning is children's time, and evenings after 9:00 P.M. are for adults. To illustrate the manner in which a target audience is covered, I rely on a personal experience. I was selected to direct a large pool (group) of herbicide commercials aimed at farmers. Rex Allen, an old-time cowboy film star and country singer was our spokesman, and we photographed all over the country. Local (not network) spots were bought in pertinent rural markets to run during supper time. After the commercials had run their schedule, sales increased dramatically.

Figure 2-1. Two major TV-commercial awards: the Clio (left) of the National Television Commercial Festival and the Lion (right) from the Cannes Film Festival.

Figure 2-2. TV-commercial awards from the Chicago Film Festival, Hollywood International Broadcasting Award, and New York's One Show Award.

PRODUCTION TECHNIQUES

A study of commercial production must consider the area of production technique. There may be some concepts that do not fit into the techniques that follow, but a high percentage does. The variations on these formats make up the bulk of television commercials.

Hidden Camera

This is a difficult type of production. Two-way mirrors, lots of footage, and more than one camera shooting at the same time so scenes intercut are only part of the problem. For legal reasons the subjects cannot know that their statements are being recorded, so hidden microphones and an expert interviewer are a must. If the commercials are used, the participants are paid at union scale and must sign a standard talent release in addition to a statement verifying the conditions of the interview. Each network has a continuity acceptance department that reviews all commercials before they are broadcast, and, if the line "hidden camera" is desired on the screen, it must be authenticated. Without this statement, some networks and stations demand that the line "a dramatization" or "a reenactment" appear on screen as a disclaimer.

"Real People" Interviews

Interviewing "real people," with the camera evident but in an inconspicuous position, is practical and effective. The selection of the people used must be carefully planned, and a number of production assistants are needed to implement the plan.

Records of everyone interviewed must be kept for later contact. Usually full payment for clearances is not made until the job has cleared the legal department and a signed statement from the person interviewed, confirming the accuracy of statement and permission to use, is obtained.

Another variation of this format is photographing individuals discussing a subject within a group. Conversation is guided by the director to cover copy points as long as the conversation sounds honest. There is a wonderful naturalness to this type of shooting because the people are comfortable with one another. The legal problems are similar to those involving interviewed subjects.

I have directed a great number of these types of commercials and have found that while the "real people" interviews require a great interviewer, group discussions need a fantastic camera operator.

Name Spokesman

Because of a celebrity's recognition value, viewers seem to attach an extraordinary value to a commercial message delivered by a star. Knowing this, the Federal Communications Commission (FCC) has recently ruled that any statements made by a famous person must be true and the proof must be made available upon request. In addition, of course, the name spokesman should be right for the subject and sales approach to make the commercial effective. The advertising agency's production business department is responsible for all contract negotiations for this type of commercial; production's concern is to shoot on the contracted days.

The FCC has also established a clear differentiation between a spokesman and an endorser. If the speaker delivers the sponsor's sales pitch or opinion, he or she is a spokesman; if it is a personal opinion, he or she is an endorser. If challenged, the sponsor must be able to back up endorsements with proof that the spokesman has used the product or service and it performed as stated. I have worked with Vincent Price on a number of commercials in which he introduced himself by name and made personal recommendations on art, home furnishings, decorating, and food. He is a recognized authority in these fields as well as a well-known personality, so he is classified as an endorser. I am also sure that the famous endorsers of American Express can authenticate their use of the charge cards. The spokesman classification applies to Robert Conrad in his battery commercials, Lorne Green with his dog food, and Orson Welles and the wine.

These rules are not legal restrictions but only guidelines set up by the FCC to protect individuals from lawsuit. Pat Boone lost a very large lawsuit because he personally recommended an acne treatment that his children had never used; the product was later proved to be ineffectual.

Slice of Life

This is a dramatic treatment of a supposed real-life situation in which product benefits are openly discussed. Although fictional, the short vignettes are supposed to give the appearance of real life. The series of commercials in which Robert Young advises his friends to drink Sanka coffee is an example of a well-known actor in a slice-of-life commercial. Procter & Gamble is a heavy user of this commercial format because its research has indicated that this format is effective for its products. Although Procter & Gamble employs a number of advertising agencies in different parts of the country, it dictates the basic approach of its commercials and tests them extensively. Many variations of this technique are written and produced and, although there is some criticism of them, they must be effective or they would be dropped. The casting for these commercials is critical; to be convincing, actors must look the part as well as read the lines.

Demonstrations

Demonstrating is an excellent method of presenting product benefits and one that truly utilizes the television medium. A visual demonstration can only be made on television or in direct selling. In addition to standard demonstrations, side-by-side demonstrations against competition have become very popular, and, if the product is right, the "torture test" is extremely effective: many automobiles have run the Baja road races and the African road rally for TV cameras to sell tires and batteries, and Timex watches have used torture tests for years. Because of the possibility of lawsuits based upon unfair labor practices, it is very important that a recognized testing service be present during production for substantiation. In all of the Sears tire and battery commercials that my company produced, the United States Testing Laboratories supervised the demonstrations. This production procedure also makes approval from the network continuity-clearance department much easier.

Minidocumentary

It takes an extremely creative production staff to squeeze a documentary into thirty seconds. This technique appears to show what is really happening without apparently using professional actors and a prepared script. By common definition, a documentary deals with some factual aspect of human society. This technique depends heavily on beautiful photography and creative editing to make it work. Sponsors of institutional advertising seem to favor the minidocumentary technique. Santa Fe, U.S. Steel, airlines, and oil companies have sponsored this type of television commercial (Figure 2-3). The director

(Courtesy Cusack Productions)

Figure 2-3. Photographing on an oil platform near the California coast for a minidocumentary produced for Santa Fe Industries.

must be able to improvise and keep flexible. A director of food and closeup work might be a catastrophe on a minidocumentary.

Product Presentation

There are two types of product-presentation commercials. Both present the product visually and describe its benefits and invisible features. The first is usually national and includes many expensively produced automobile commercials. The other group is usualy locally produced and utilizes still pictures and merchandise close-ups accompanied by a strong announcer. The latter are basically radio commercials that show the product, and they have proven to be very effective, particularly in direct-response advertising. Many mail-order record and appliance companies use this type of commercial, and manufacturers supply them to retail outlets for local retail advertising. As Robert Knapp, a television pioneer and former vice-president of Campbell Ewald Advertising, once told me, "Sometimes you can't beat a title slide."

Contemporary

Since television commercials were first broadcast there have been techniques to achieve a departure from anything previously produced. These "trendy" commercials were quickly copied if they seemed successful. The latest of this group seems to be the high-tech spots that incorporate exaggerated colors, costumes, backgrounds, sound tracks, and acting. They also use many video-generated visual effects and a high percentage of computer animation. RC Cola, automobiles, cosmetics, and even Timex watches use the glowing colors, orange skies, art deco sets, and stylized design that identify the contemporary-style commercial. The lasting quality and sales effectiveness of these commercials remains to be determined.

Animation

Animation means "bringing to life." Because some concepts are difficult to film in live action, the agency may choose animation. Animation may also be used to attract attention or to entertain. Cross-sections of animated stomachs and lungs, for example, illustrate the magic results of medication, and little bugs scream "Raid" to entertain. Computer-controlled animation stands have created a completely new type of animation. Formerly, an animation cameraman was needed to take every individual picture that makes up an animated sequence. Now a computer can move the camera and make the exposures according to its preset program and repeat the identical action as many times as needed. The result is the streaking lettering and multicolored trails of logotypes that are so common on television commercials today; this is sometimes referred to as slit-scan or laser animation. Computers are also used in conjunction with video-generated graphics. Because this type of animation eliminates drawing time, it saves both time and money. Although traditional character animation using individual drawings costs a considerable amount of money, the savings in oncamera residual payments to live performers can be very substantial. (There are more details about this on page 36.)

Stop Motion

This is a specialized type of animation. Individual exposures are taken of three-dimensional objects; the objects are moved slightly for each exposure. When projected at twenty-four frames per second (standard projector speed), the objects seem to come to life. The puppet animation of the Pillsbury Dough Boy, Speedy Alka Seltzer, Swiss Miss, and the Handy Helper are made in this manner. Client products have frequently come to life, marching, talking, and reacting through the use of stop motion. This is time-consuming work that is produced by a limited number of production companies in the United States and Europe. Stop-motion animation can be combined with live action during postproduction (see pages 94–96).

Hand Puppets

Hand puppets have been around for centuries, but the Muppets have created an entirely new school of design and manipulation. Imitators and former associates have organized companies to make commercials using this approach. The puppeteer's ability to view the performance while manipulating has been a great help. Many TV monitors are used so that each puppeteer has a monitor available to check the action from the camera's angle. Videotape recorders are used for immediate playback. This is one of the less expensive production techniques.

Limbo

The word *limbo* is frequently used in scripts to mean a background that is not identifiable. The word itself means "oblivion," and its use in a script to describe a background must be interpreted for the practicalities of production. It is generally accepted in production that limbo means a simple shadowless background that could be anywhere. A neutral color is sometimes used, but, as a general rule, it is a shade of gray. Long shots in limbo are usually photographed on a painted sweep, a set where the floor blends (sweeps) into the wall. This is to avoid the break between the two surfaces, as this horizon indication would bring the scene back to undesired reality. A sweep background is usually a floor-and-rear-wall combination of many floor-to-wall and wall-to-wall sweeps that give a feeling of infinity in every direction.

On this limbo background, almost anything can be staged. Presenter commercials are frequently photographed on a limbo background. The nowhere of the limbo background is used for automobiles, furniture, and a wide range of merchandise. Large groups of people such as garment-union workers, insurance agents, and real-estate agents sing their jingles in this unidentifiable place.

Special Effects

This term usually refers to the highly technical optical effects made on an optical bench (see Chapter 5, pages 94–96), but some types of special effects must be made during original photography.

Slow motion: This gives the slow, sensuous look to the scene of two people running through the fields to embrace one another. It permits a longer-than-usual look at action and is frequently used to heighten dramatic moments. It is achieved by shooting at a higher frame per second (fps) speed than the normal standard projector's 24 fps. When a scene is photographed at speeds from 72 fps to 150 fps and projected at standard speed, slow motion results. A regular camera with a high-speed motor can achieve this effect.

Time lapse: This is the opposite of slow motion. For this result the camera is run at a much slower speed than the projector's 24 fps. Time is compressed with this photography; as clouds rapidly billow, people scurry about, and in thirty seconds a complete day can be shown from one viewpoint.

High speed: As confusing as this may seem, high speed is actually extreme slow motion. Special cameras are needed to show the contents of the Contac capsule spilling out. The corona of a drop of liquid as it hits a surface is a perfect example of high-speed photography: it is photographed at 2,000 fps.

Special lenses: These are used for some unusual visuals. Extremely short (bug eye) lenses are used to distort images by exaggerating perspective while maintaining sharp focus throughout the frame. Very long lenses seem to remove depth and perspective and bring an object close while permitting a background to be out of focus. Zoom lenses permit the changing of focal length while the camera is shooting.

Special filters: These are placed in front of the camera lens for a number of reasons. To give a foggy appearance to a scene, a fog filter can be used. The beautiful soft glamorous look of the typical cosmetic commercial is helped by diffusion filters. A star filter makes every white highlight on a picture look like a star. Even contrast and color can be controlled by a filter. A good photographer has all these filters, and more.

Special Photography

A large percentage of television commercial photography is unconventional. The scripts and storyboards demand more than the standard well-exposed, well-lit, and eye-level camera work. Sometimes a novel camera angle and unusual equipment is called for.

Unique Viewpoints

Because a television commercial is competing for attention against other commercials and programs, it must sometimes resort to unusual camera viewpoints. These viewpoints cannot be attained with such standard camera-support equipment as tripods, dollies, cranes, or even human hands.

Helicopter: Air-to-ground and air-to-air photographs are usually taken from a helicopter and have become specialties. Many important elements in this type of commercial must be covered to assure good footage; therefore, the agency should pick a production company with experience in this area. Full insurance coverage for the cameraman is imperative. Many eager cameramen are willing to attempt helicopter photography without special insurance, but such flying is classified as high risk and will sometimes void a standard policy. Andrew Costikyan, one of the best helicopter cameramen in the business, will not shoot from a helicopter without seeing a death-and-disability insurance policy made out for the specific project. This is the production company's responsibility.

An experienced helicopter cameraman knows the best pilots, choppers, and camera system for the required work. The standard camera equipment used is an Arriflex 16-mm or 35-mm with 400-foot magazines and a zoom lens (Figure 2-4). The chopper must be powerful enough to perform difficult, critical maneuvers; the pilot must be able to understand the cameraman's requirements; the camera mount must be properly installed and balanced to isolate the camera from vibration. And with costs more than $500 an hour for the helicopter and pilot, the weather must not only be clear but free of gusts. A helicopter and pilot usually charge for air time only, with a minimum charge for standby ground time.

Helicopter shooting is used for many automobile running shots, travel advertising, and any visuals that need a view from the air. A properly set-up helicopter is an ideal aerial camera platform with extreme flexibility.

Underwater: This style of spot calls for clear water, the proper equipment, and expert personnel. To find clear water, it may be necessary to travel thousands of miles. This travel is complicated by the fact that all equipment is bulky and needs more than the normal amount of support gear (Figure 2-5). Most underwater cameras are standard 35-mm or 16-mm models completely enclosed in a waterproof case that permits access to all camera controls, with viewing and shooting parts that are optically ground. The camera assembly must be able to be adjusted for neutral buoyancy so that it can be easily handled under water. Since water has the optical qualities of a lens and magnifies all objects by about a third, most underwater work is photographed with wide-angle lenses. The additional benefit of the wide-angle lens is that it reduces the distance between subject and camera, thus reducing the amount of water-suspended impurities that can degrade a picture.

Figure 2-4. A 16-mm Arriflex mounted on a Continental helicopter rig in a Jet Ranger.

Figure 2-5. Underwater photography for a Reynolds Aluminum commercial; in the background is the Aluminaut, a diving research vehicle. The camera is a 35-mm unit designed by the cameraman.

Underwater lighting is very basic, but the crew must be skilled. Although it is rarely necessary to dive below fifty feet, the crew should all be certified divers and be thoroughly knowledgeable in underwater production. Deep water is extremely blue and dark even above fifty feet; therefore, it is only practical to work in the middle of the day when the sun is high and needs to penetrate the least possible amount of water. This viewpoint can be used in almost any commercial calling for an unusual visual. The dangerous excitement of the Andrea Doria treasure recovery was used for Budweiser beer. Soap, aluminum, travel services, water softeners, and purifiers have all used an underwater viewpoint. Plenty of air tanks and a good compressor are the number-two requirement of a successful underwater shoot; the number-one requirement is the most experienced cameraman you can employ.

Steadicam: Many scenes call for a hand-held camera because of limited work area, intricacy of camera movement, or first-person viewpoint. Since man has two legs that must be used as alternate camera platforms, a camera mount has been invented that smooths out the bumpy movements of the hand-held shot. Called the Steadicam, it is a well-balanced camera mount that is attached to the cameraman (Figure 2-6). It combines the flexibility of a hand-held camera with the smoothness of a dolly. This is the only way that a camera can move continuously and smoothly around corners, through small doorways, even up stairs. This type of mount seems to be frequently used in housewife-presenter commercials, but can also be used to smooth out any photography that might otherwise be bumpy.

A video-assist monitor is used with this camera mount because the camera must be steady and the operator cannot keep his eye to the camera eyepiece because of head movement while walking. Steadicam-type mounts demand a very strong, experienced operator. Panavision and Continental systems manufacture a similar mount

Figure 2-6. The Universal Model Steadicam with a CP-16R 16-mm Reflex camera.

for film and video cameras; Steadicam was the original.

Another procedure for stabilizing hand-held photography is also available. This involves the use of gyroscope stabilizers, small motors that are mounted vertically and horizontally on the hand-held camera to maintain equilibrium. It is almost impossible to make an uneven move with this method, but it does add a few pounds to the weight.

Snorkel: The Kenworthy Snorkel camera system appears to be an inverted periscope attached to a standard camera (Figure 2-7). The benefits of this system are fairly evident in situations where the total room needed for photography can be measured in inches. Remote viewing through a video monitor is used. The viewpoint position can move between actors, completely around small bottles and other objects, and through a labyrinth of small items even at surface level because the diameter of the periscope tube is only a few inches. The Snorkel has found its greatest use in television commercials, for it can move to within inches of featured products and continuously integrate them into other elements of the commercial. The familiar tracking shot through a maze of small bottles ending up with a big closeup of the hero product is only one example of this capability. The Snorkel system must be mounted on support equipment such as dollies, cranes, and rigs. The periscope optical tubes vary in size from eighteen inches to six feet.

Special rigging: The rapid construction of any unusual support system for camera, lights, or crew is the domain of the rigger. Traditional methods of photography are sometimes impossible under prevailing conditions. The problem can be explained to a top-grade rigger and in moments a solution emerges. Riggers are problem solvers, and their whole world seems to be made up of suction cups, guy wires, angle irons, aluminum conduit, and plywood.

A simple rig might require suction-cupping a camera to a car fender for running shots of a tire or a viewpoint from inside a crashing car (Figure 2-8). More complicated are the camera platforms that hang on the outside of

(Courtesy Kenworthy Camera Systems, Inc.)

Figure 2-7. The Kenworthy Snorkel System. This setup includes a 35-mm Arriflex, video monitor, crane, and periscope assembly.

Figure 2-8. Rigging a 35-mm Arriflex for running shots of tires. *Right to left*: the cameraman, assistant cameraman, and rigger.

vehicles, buildings, or sheer precipices. If there is no standard equipment that will put a camera where the director wants it, it is time to call in a rigger.

Table Top

Table-top photography is a film specialty that originated with television commercials. It includes any type of closeup photography and usually means food setups. In the early television days this type of filming was referred to as insert shooting because it could be done on a small insert stage using a few crewmen by a special-effects company. Table-top filming still uses a small crew, and many production companies handle only this type of work.

Food photography not only needs expert closeup lighting and camera work, it also requires extremely capable home economists and stylists. The same rare food-preparation ability needed for national magazine advertising is necessary for the photography in television advertising. The Federal Trade Commission (FTC) has ruled that the advertised product itself must be used in the commercial; no substitutes are permitted. Before this ruling it was possible to cheat in the preparation of attractive food setups. The stylist has therefore become an important member of the table-top crew. The accessories chosen by a good stylist add immeasurably to any table-top photography.

Many advertising agencies lean heavily on their own art directors in this type of commercial. The art director sometimes selects the home economist and stylist and works closely with them during production. Still photographers have made very strong inroads in this type of production.

Animation Techniques

Animation is any motion picture produced frame-by-frame, and this definition includes not only the familiar cartoons but the title and client logotype scenes (whether stationary, zooming, or glittering with stars) that conclude the vast majority of commercials.

Animation is particularly successful in television commercials because it offers the agency total control over what appears on the screen. Gone are the fussy child and animal performers; vanished is the chorus-line dancer who cannot keep in step. Animation is usually a two-dimensional world where weather contingencies never prevail and shadows and flares never spoil takes. All the exigencies of a live shoot are controlled by an artist's pencil and, although the animation process can be expensive and time-consuming, no one ever paid a cartoon character residuals.

Television-commercial animation can be broken down into three general classifications: illustration (character animation), graphic design, and special effects.

Illustration animation: Illustration animation creates worlds, the settings and inhabitants of which are rendered in manners that vary from extreme realism to extreme stylization (Figure 2-9). This type of animation owes most of its success and technical sophistication to Walt Disney Productions, which fathered an entire generation of animators, many of whom worked in commercial production. The Disney studios perfected the relation of sound to image and the production-line techniques that have become the industry standard.

The production line always starts with the script; then a storyboard is made and the art directors design the characters, rendering them in full detail. The sound track, with appropriate character voices, is recorded. The animators then time the sound track frame-by-frame for voice, action, sound cues, and music.

Next comes the pencil test. After the sound track is broken down into timings for the scenes of action, the animators draw extreme points in the action on pencil tissues. Then the "in-betweeners" make additional pencil tissues of all the intermediate action between the extremes. When a sequence is completely sketched, it is photographed one frame at a time according to the instructions on a frame-count list. After development, the film is projected at standard speed. This pencil test is the checkpoint for the action, just as the art director's renderings are the checkpoint for character depiction. To make changes after these points involves considerable expense. The test should be projected interlocked with the sound track; any corrections and comments are incorporated in the final drawing.

The finishing stages are started by cleaning up the roughly rendered tissues and adding all necessary character details. These drawings are then duplicated onto clear acetate film called cells (originally cellophane was used, hence the name). The backs of the cells are painted with opaque color that adheres to the acetate. Backgrounds, which can range from the simplicity of a single color to the complexity of a photorealistic landscape, are painted on paper or board. Tissues, cells, and backgrounds are hung from the same pegs to insure alignment. When all painting has been completed, each cell is placed over the proper background and photographed. The figures always seem to be on their own plane because the opaque color blocks out the background completely, and multiple cells are frequently used for each frame.

Figure 2-9. A single frame from a character-animation commercial; this is a standard ink-and-paint type animation used for the 3M Corporation commercial "A Slow Death to Crabgrass."

The final film is projected at twenty-four frames per second.

Because television commercials must always attempt to attract attention, new methods of illustration continually evolve. Drawing techniques are limited only by the artist's imagination. The characters in illustration animation can also be created sculpturally by using wooden or clay puppets that are moved a fraction of an inch for every frame photographed; at standard projection speed they appear to move of their own power. This is stop-motion photography (see page 30); the George Pal puppetoons and many commercials have been made in this manner.

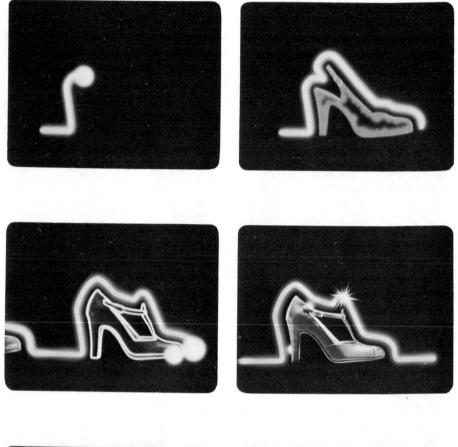

Figure 2-10. A TV commercial for the Wohl shoe company combining live action and design animation. Animated on an aerial-image animation stand.

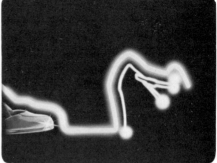
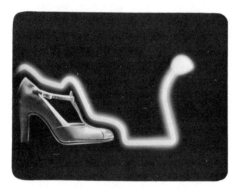
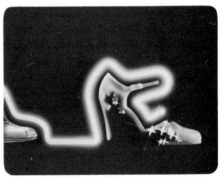

(Courtesy Goldsholl Associates, Northfield, Illinois)

Graphic-design animation: Graphic design in animation came of age in the late 1950s; the theatrical titles of Saul Bass on the West Coast come to mind, and Mort Goldscholl in the Midwest and the Ferro Brothers on the East Coast also did pioneer work. Whereas the illustration animators came from cinematic backgrounds, the graphic-design animators came from print art direction. Theirs is a world of shape, color, line, hue, texture, and movement; and these elements exist in a pure or abstract way. The means are not top-lit painted cells but Kodaliths, colored gels, and bottom-lit light boxes. The titles and logos that come at the end of many commercials are part of this tradition; they use approaches that can vary from the primitive to the sophisticated (Figure 2-10).

The invention of the computer-controlled animation stand advanced the ease of shooting graphic effects; it made the laser, streak, metal, glow, and sparkle effects more convenient. Before the computer-controlled stand, the camerman in addition to changing the artwork, had to individually set every move of the camera and the section holding the artwork. Now the same scene can be made by feeding the problem into the computer and letting it run the stand (Figure 2-11). By programming the moves of a complete cycle, the identical camera moves are automatically repeated. The individual cells must still be changed by hand, however.

It is worth noting that almost any effect shot on a computer animation stand can be shot on a standard one. The computer stand could cost three times as much, but the regular stand may triple the shooting time. The difference is that the computer reduces the tedium and the time for the cameraman. If the effect involves artwork changes during the camera moves, then a regular stand may be able to do the task as quickly as a computer stand.

Computer-generated and computer-enhanced images have aided graphic animation, but what is crucial is the talent of the designer who operates or commands the computer (Figure 2-12).

Special-effects animation: Special-effects animation evolved from graphic-design animation, but in many sophisticated commercials, such as the Bob Abel classics for Seven-Up, it is difficult to tell where the graphic elements leave off and the photographic elements begin. Special-effects animation implies no particular style. Generally, it is the use of animation in conjunction with live photography, computer-generated graphics, or any other film elements that make for a special visual effect.

This is a complicated world with refined standards of operation all its own; some of its modes of operation will be explained in the section in Chapter 5 devoted to optical houses. But special effects in its simplest sense is the combination of live-action footage with animation, and there are situations in studio production where the problems of combining these must be solved.

There are two methods of producing a combination of animation and live action on film. The most common in-

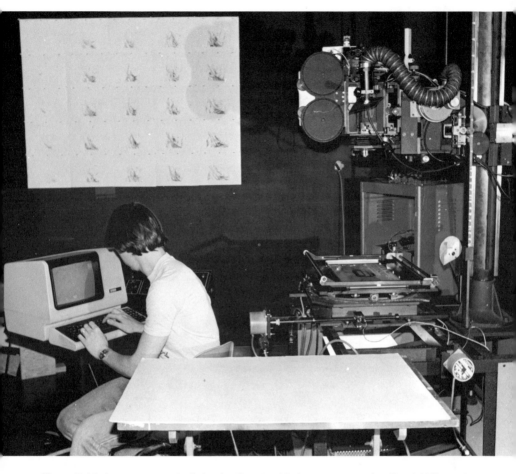

Figure 2-11. A computer-controlled animation stand being programmed at Special Effects, Inc.

volves the optical bench during postproduction; the photography and animation are supplied to an optical company, which then combines them on one negative (see Chapter 5, pages 91–94). It is important to check with an optical company or postproduction service before proceeding with production to ascertain what elements will be needed to complete the work. The other popular method of combining animation and live photography is on an aerial-image animation stand. This work is done by an animation company rather than an optical house. Drawings on clear cells are photographed over their corresponding frame of projected live action. Cartoon

(Courtesy Special Effects, Inc.)

Figure 2-12. A TV spot with streak effects, one of many computerized results that can be achieved with a single piece of artwork.

figures on screen with live actors are sometimes animated in this manner with a saving of both time and money.

Stop-Motion Photography

Stop-motion photography, sometimes known as single-frame photography, has a long history. It is very popular with student filmmakers who have their first camera. A sequence of pictures is taken one frame at a time over a period of time. These frames are then projected at the 24 fps, and the results can be quite exciting. Fruit can dance around a table, clay figures may seem to walk, and sand can assume weird shapes (Figure 2-13).

(Courtesy Goldsholl Associates, Inc., Northfield, Illinois)

Pixillation is used to describe a category of stop motion in which actors rather than inanimate objects are photographed. Between exposures the actors are manipulated so they appear to do unusual or impossible feats when the film is projected at standard speed. In the early 1970s a group of commercials was made for an oil company that showed a family zipping around streets on the seats of their pants. They stopped for red lights, turned corners, came to a stop, and stood up, all through the magic of the single-frame exposure. Most film historians credit Norman McLaren of the Canadian Film Bureau with originating the technique in the 1940s. Since that time it has been used on a multitude of commercials; it is a type of animation.

There are many fine animation studios all over the country. New York and Los Angeles appear to have the bulk of them, but there are many small studios in other areas. In selecting an animation studio to produce a commercial, careful studies of samples are imperative. Character design and cleanliness of shooting should be carefully studied, and the permanently employed staff evaluated. A pencil test should always be run; this indicates the caliber of the final job. Good animation is expensive and takes time.

←

Figure 2-13. Production of a Hamburger Helper commercial that uses stop-motion technique; Helping Hand is a registered trademark of General Mills, Inc., and is used here with permission.

CHAPTER

PREPRODUCTION

After approval of scripts and story-boards, the agency proceeds with the preparations for shooting the commercials; this phase is called preproduction. Meetings between the account, media, creative, management, and production departments consolidate all information relative to the project. An accurate estimate of the campaign cost, including all elements, must be made for final client approval. At this point an agency producer is usually assigned to the production; his or her job is to oversee the making of the commercial.

It is important to remember that every advertising agency has its own organization. A very small agency might have one person performing a number of functions. In many cases free-lance people are hired to help staff an agency during production, and business-management companies can be hired to handle payroll, contracts, and talent and residual payments.

PRODUCTION DETAILS

The bulk of this work is done by the agency's TV-commercial producer and, if the agency is staffed fully, by the broadcast business manager in conjunction with the producer. Most creative departments keep in close touch with production during the preproduction phase. Producers are sometimes assigned to work exclusively for one creative group, and at other times they operate from an independent production department under a manager or executive producer.

Broadcast Business

In addition to the business and accounting departments, many agencies that deal largely with television commercials have set up a production business or a broadcast business department. Some very large agencies have both departments, with production business responsible for the financial aspects up to the broadcast and the broadcast business responsible for all money matters after broadcast. This department is usually responsible for the internal administration of all production dollars, including agency funds used for experimenting in new techniques as well as client production dollars. This includes all basic bids, revision costs, and any other cost that might be incurred. Among the many responsibilities assigned to a production-business manager are the following:

- Assist the producer on bidding instructions between the agency and the production company
- Coordinate production schedules and prepare advance production cost estimates
- Review studio costs with the agency producer; after the studio recommendation has been determined, clear the studio costs through the account group
- Coordinate commercial talent negotiations, including inquiries, availabilities, negotiations, auditions, screen tests and contracts, use of minority talent
- Secure proper legal and network clearance if the agency does not have its own legal department
- Be responsible for communications with clients and account groups on the business aspects of production (costs, additional billing, legal problems, personnel changes)
- Prepare and control talent-reuse budgets based on media plan and number of commercials
- Interpret and apply union codes

The Agency Producer

The person usually assigned to supervise the production of television commercials for the advertising agency is the agency producer. This is not the same job as a studio producer. The studio producer is deeply involved in every detail of production and is not directly employed by the advertising agency; the agency producer is strictly a supervisor who insures the agency of an acceptable final product.

In some advertising agencies the producer is part of broadcast business because cost control is a major concern. However, most agencies feel that creative work is far more important than cost and therefore include the producer as part of the creative department. There is no standard in the advertising industry, but Jackson Phelps, vice-president and director of production services of the J. Walter Thompson Agency in Chicago, has defined the job of the agency producer in the following manner:

The agency producer is the agency's "orchestra leader." He or she is responsible for studio recommendations, cost/bid preparation and analysis, organizing and supervising and preproduction meetings, casting reviews, set discussions, budget, schedules. The producer is the agency's voice to the studio on all business and creative matters. The prime concern—creatively—is to determine and then shape creative needs of the commercial by assembling a team of studio specialists to carry out the creative needs. He or she is the translator for the creative people, legal, and client on all policy matters at all stages of production from prebid through final client approval of the answer print.

The above job description certainly indicates the difficulty the agency producers have in keeping everyone happy and productive. It is a specialized occupation with many demands. The producer is usually the most technically knowledgeable person representing the agency and functions as production watchdog. Responsibility for budget and schedule usually resides with the producer, and the creative aspects remain with the writer or art director.

Since the creative department has such a strong concern about its commercials, there are agency job descriptions such as writer-producer and art director–producer. This varies from agency to agency. Recently there has been a trend toward using free-lance producers for supervision. This has both economic and practical benefits because a free-lancer is usually knowledgeable and can be dismissed when a production is completed. Many agency producers are former art directors or writers and understand the complete picture of broadcast-commercial production.

SAG and AFTRA

The performers' labor organizations in the broadcast industry are the American Federation of Radio and Television Artists (AFTRA) and the Screen Actors Guild (SAG). AFTRA has jurisdiction over radio, live television, and videotape; the guild has responsibility for film performers. The Screen Extras Guild (SEG) represents extras and is a consideration on some commercials. Most advertising agencies and production companies are signatories to pay and working-condition agreements with these unions.

Rates for both organizations are basically the same. A session or performance fee is paid to the on-camera or off-camera principals, and additional fees are paid for use and reuse. These fees are based on the number of cities covered by the advertisement and by the number of times it is shown. Cities are rated by population. It is informative to project talent costs for a thirty-second commercial with two on-camera actors and one announcer. Because rates are always changing and pension, health, and welfare costs

must also be considered, I have used approximate 1981 figures for this budget estimate:

Talent costs of nonnetwork television spot with two on-camera performers and one announcer, to be used in four markets including Los Angeles, New York, and Chicago for 13 weeks.

Session fee, 2 on-camera principals (8-hour session), $275 each	$550.00
On-camera fee for use in NY, LA, Chicago, and one extra market at $978.45 per performer, less the original session payment of $275.00	$1406.90
Off-camera announcer (2-hour session)	$206.80
Off-camera fee for NY, LA, Chicago and one extra market at $690.53, less original payment of $206.80	$483.73
Total talent payment	$2647.43
Pension and welfare payment (10%) to SAG	$264.74
Total cost of talent	$2912.17

The session fee is a down payment for use. Network commercials are charged for by the number of plays. A classification for dealer commercials is also available; this type of commercial is cleared for a six-month period to be used only by dealers on a station-by-station basis.

Reuse payments fall under the descriptive terms of residuals. The session fee is paid for the performance itself, and the residuals are paid to the performer whenever the commercial is used. There is also a holding fee that can be paid to a performer; this acts as a residual payment by prohibiting the player from making any commercials for a competitive product. In fact, a residual payment is for work that the performer must turn down. Before this type of payment was specified by the SAG, the same person might demonstrate and sell many competitive products and inform the audience that each one was the best. For example, in the early days of television I used the same excellent demonstrator extolling the virtues of Westinghouse, Admiral, and Bendix clothes washers on commercials that were broadcast back-to-back. This cannot happen today.

Even when using nonprofessional talent, as on interview or minidocumentary spots, the agency pays the identical SAG fee; the performer does not need to be a member in good standing of the guild for the first performance. A Taft-Hartley release form is usually signed by the artist in this instance; this form specifies that this is a first performance and that if any further performances are to be made, the performer agrees to join the guild. The so-called right-to-work provision of the Taft-Hartley Act makes this procedure possible.

In addition to performers' contracts, the business department is also concerned with supplier contract and payments. The standard schedule for the production of TV commercials calls for payment of one-third on start of production, one-third on completion of main photography, and the balance on delivery of an approved answer print, a fully corrected picture-and-sound print. This payment schedule makes it important to select a financially solid production company. Many production companies would not be able to complete a project if a major accident occurred. Accidents like X-ray fogging of film at airports during a bomb inspection, camera malfunction, laboratory malfunction, or customs delays can and have happened (to me). It is sometimes necessary to procure production insurance to protect everyone against such a contingency. Insurance is available from many agents who specialize in such coverage; premiums will, of course, match the risk.

Legal Clearance

Because of consumer-advocate pressure and the lawsuit potential, legal clearance has become a major concern of anyone connected with broadcast advertising. Since the federal government has the authority to grant and take away broadcast frequency, it is imperative that its rules and regulations be closely observed. The Federal Communications Commission (FCC) is the regulatory body for all broadcasting and decides if a television station is operating in the public interest. The Federal Trade Commission (FTC) has the power to investigate business activities and issue a complaint against any company considered to be practicing unfair competition or other violations of trade laws and codes. The FTC works closely with the FCC in matters relating to broadcasting.

In addition to the FCC and FTC, other federal agencies are also interested in television advertising; the Food and Drug Administration (FDA) and the Postal Service are two examples. The FDA is concerned about the accuracy of drug advertising and the Postal Service is concerned with mail fraud. Many states have enacted legislation dealing with specific groups of products advertised on television, and better business bureaus and parent teacher organizations also have a large voice.

The larger advertising agencies have found it necessary to have their own legal departments, although most agencies either use outside legal sources when needed or check with stations to make sure that there is nothing in a proposed commercial that might make them liable for a lawsuit.

After a commercial has been approved but before production starts, the proposed script and storyboard should be sent to the continuity department of the network that is part of the advertising plan. If a station-to-station time buy is contemplated, the script should be cleared by the larger affiliates of the network. To assure the self-regulation of broadcasters, an association has been created to interpret all the FCC regulations and publish them as a code for their members. This is the National Association of Broadcasters (NAB).

The NAB has established a television code that its members are obliged to honor. This code sets the standard for programs and commercial material that can be broadcast by its members stations. Many elements of this code are subject to individual interpretation, for each station or network insists upon the right of acceptance of a commercial. The code must be considered when creating or producing a television commercial.

The NAB television code establishes responsibilities for advertisers, broadcasters, and even viewers. It also establishes standards for all programming and commercials. One important standard relates to quantity and placement of such nonprogram material as commercials, promotional announcements, billboards, and short visualized announcements of program sponsorship before and after the actual program: for every sixty-minute period during prime time (three consecutive hours designated by each station between 6:00 P.M. and 10:00 P.M.), nonprogram material may not exceed nine minutes and thirty seconds. In non-prime time, up to sixteen minutes of any sixty minutes can be nonprogram material.

The number of program interruptions is also specified in the NAB code; prime time should have no more than two interruptions per thirty minutes, but other time can have up to four breaks. News, sports, weather, and special events are exempt from these standards because of their nature.

There are guidelines that pertain to competitive advertising, lotteries and contests, nonprescription drugs, vegetable oils and margarines, and many others. Guidelines for alcoholic beverages include details of how beer and wine must be presented (it is never actually drunk).

Children's advertising has extremely strict controls placed on it. The NAB feels that everyone involved in the creation, production, and presentation of advertising to children has a responsibility to assure that such material avoids exploiting a child's developing cognitive ability and sense of values. Because of parent pressure, the FCC, FTC, and NAB are especially concerned with television advertising to children. The NAB has pages of guidelines on this subject.

PREBID SESSION

When the scripts and storyboards have been approved by client, creative, continuity, and legal, they are ready for production. All interested individuals meet before the boards are presented to the production companies for bidding. A good record of this meeting should be kept, because many of the people there will not see the commercial again until after editing has been completed. This record can be incorporated into the specifications given to the production companies that bid on the job. The basic concept of the spot and all artistic and mechanical requirements are carefully spelled out in these production notes. Bidders receive identical sets of notes so all production estimates are based on the same specifications.

Usually three bidders are asked to estimate the production of a television commercial, but narrowing the choice down to these three is sometimes time consuming. Sample reels or ¾-inch cassettes are requested from any production company with the staff (director, cameraman, producer) that seems

right for the project. Types of samples that conform in general to the proposed commercial are usually specified. These could be dialogue, children, food, location, low-key (a style of photography that has a dark appearance because of heavy shadows and minimal lighting), high-key (photography that is very bright and shadowless), cosmetics, cars, comedy, and music. The success of current commercials is also considered when choosing a potential bidder. Most production companies have a representative; the word *salesperson* is rarely used when referring to the "rep." The rep represents talent—not only actors but also directors and cameramen—and tries to keep a high profile in the industry for the person or company represented.

After a general screening of samples, specific production companies are asked to submit written bids based on script, storyboards, production notes, and a bid meeting.

BIDDING

The first decision regarding a commercial is its method of production—film or videotape. Most large advertising agencies prefer film production for their commercials. There are many reasons for this preference; the most common is the ability to screen the edited work print (the print made from the original negative) before a final judgment is made. Many individuals can share in the decision making and corrections are very easy to accomplish. Videotape is not easy to correct; each correction is almost a complete reedit. The "film look" is also important to many advertisers; there seems to be a much softer look to pictures that originate on film. Also, film cameramen are much more experienced in lighting. Videotape is sharper but seems a bit "raw" to many people.

Another benefit of film is the ability to show sample reels. Reels are the resumes of the industry, although with the proliferation of video players, this need is diminishing.

The production department screens sample reels on a continuing basis and when it decides to produce on film, it usually has a number of suggestions. The creative department also has some definite opinions because of current success stories and reels that they have seen. At least three producers will be asked to bid on the project after a review of the selected director's sample reels. All three bidders should be acceptable to the agency; the final choice will be based on the director (his or her talent, reputation, and fee), price, producer's reliability, schedule, and location.

Most production estimates are very competitive, but there are times when this is not true. A large variation in price could be caused by a director's fee. Most directors charge for their services on a per-day basis. Pre- and postproduction are sometimes included, or they might be extra. The fee should be specified on an Association of Independent Commercial Producers (AICP) cost-breakdown sheet that has become standard in bidding procedures (Figure 3-1). Depending on the director's desirability, this fee ranges from $500 to $5,000 per day.

A typical production-company mark-up is 35 percent of cost excluding director's fee, but this can vary depending upon the business on hand. Experience with an advertising agency can also affect the markup, because some agencies insist upon much higher production values than others. The amount of time scheduled to shoot a job also determines cost. This is one of the biggest problems in production estimates, as the reasons for extending a shooting schedule are always questionable.

Another type of bid that is in vogue is the cost plus fixed fee. This means that after a bid is accepted, no more markups are permitted. All changes must be authorized and no profit is permitted on these changes. Once the project has started, the producer works with a fixed amount of markup. Many times it is best to have all companies figure on the same specified schedule and make an allowance for any extra days of shooting on a cost-plus basis. Whatever price is quoted, it is always wise to allow a 10 percent contingency in the budget for production.

Schedule is a budgetary consideration because overtime might accumulate and also because conflicts (for example, a booking on another project) may arise. Location is a major factor in determining price; some production companies have agreements with firms in other areas in order to produce efficiently without the huge expense of transporting a great number of people.

Since any costs incurred by the production company are marked up 35 percent, it is a good idea for the adver-

(Courtesy Association of Independent Commercial Producers)

Association of Independent Commercial Producers, Inc.

TELEVISION COMMERCIAL PRODUCTION

STUDIO COST SUMMARY

Date:

Production Co:		Agency:	Agency job #
Address:		Client:	Product:
Telephone No.:	Job #		
Production Contact:		Agency prod:	Tel:
Director:		Agency art dir:	Tel:
Cameraman:		Agency writer:	Tel:
Set Designer:		Agency Bus. Mgr:	Tel:
Editor:		Commercial title:	No. Length:
No. pre-prod. days	pre-light/rehearse	1.	
No. build/strike days	Hours:	2.	
No. Studio shoot days	Hours:	3.	
No. Location days	Hours:	4.	
Location sites:		Agency supplies:	

SUMMARY OF ESTIMATED PRODUCTION COSTS					
1. Pre-production and wrap costs	Totals A and C				
2. Shooting crew labor	Total B				
3. Studio costs: Build / shoot / strike	Totals D, E, and F				
4. Location travel and expenses	Total G				
5. Equipment costs	Total H				
6. Film stock develop and print: No. feet	Total I				
7. Props, wardrobe, animals	Total J				
8. Director/Creative fees	Total K				
9. Payroll taxes, P & W and misc.	Total L				
10. Insurance					
11.	**Sub-Total - Direct costs**				
12. Mark-up (% of direct costs)					
13. Talent costs and expenses	Total M and N				
14. Editorial / Videotape	Total O and P				
15.	**Grand Total**				
16. Weather day					
17.					
18.					

Comments:

Figure 3-1. The standard AICP bid form used for most television-commercial estimates.

tising agency to do a portion of the production work and pay some bills directly, rather than through the production company. This is particularly true in the casting of commercials. A casting service works directly with an agency, not through a production company. Performers can be paid directly through their agents, saving the production-company markup.

As part of his preproduction services, the director should be present at final castings. Some directors insist not only on being present at all casting sessions but also in supervising them. This arrangement depends on the agency and the production company. Big-name performers should always be paid directly by the agency, not only to save money, but also because special contracts must be arranged directly between the agency (and perhaps the advertiser) and the star. There are times when the advertising agency can supply the location, which saves production time and money. Client-owned locations, are a tremendous help in saving construction expenses; McDonalds, Standard Oil, and many other chain operations have installations that are used exclusively for photography. Wardrobe, props, and even air fare can be arranged for and paid for by an agency, if it has a staff available. These production elements should be listed on bid sheets as "supplied by the agency" and also detailed in any list of production requirements.

The agency must request a price for cancelling the shooting if there is a chance of a late holdup or postponement. If exterior shooting is part of the production, the bid should include a weather-day price. Weather reports are not perfect; what would the cost be if it rains or snows in the middle of shooting (Figure 3-2)? Everyone comes back the next day to finish and earns a second day's pay, but should a full markup be attached to the second day? All these questions should be answered in the bid.

Specifications

A bidder must know requirements to prepare an accurate bid. The first specification should be size of film stock. Both 35-mm and 16-mm width film stock can be used for production; 35-mm film is three times more expensive to use than 16-mm. Ten minutes of 16-mm film is 360 feet, while the same amount of time in 35-mm is 900 feet. Also, 35-mm film costs more per foot and laboratory costs are higher for developing and printing; but the quality of 35-mm production can rarely be matched in 16-mm. The steadiness of image available in 35-mm is a requirement if sophisticated optical effects are to be introduced in postproduction. For low budget commercials 16-mm is excellent and the equipment used is not only cheaper to buy or rent but it is also very portable and easy to use.

The 35-mm cameras most used in 35-mm production are Panavision, Arriflex, and Mitchell, the workhorses in standard production. There are many manufacturers of fine 16-mm cameras, although most professionals use Arriflex, Eclair, CPC, Aaton, or the old reliable Mitchells (Figures 3-3 through 3-7). The camerman must use a camera

Figure 3-2. Waiting for weather. A BNC Mitchell camera mounted on a Chapman Titan crane in the back lot of the Burbank Studios.

that he trusts. Special equipment such as cranes, dollies, and wind machines must be specified. Very few production companies own their own camera equipment; it is generally rented for each job.

The type of sound expected must be stated. Synchronous (sync) sound means sound taken while shooting, such as dialogue or actual sound ef-fects; it calls for a quiet camera, special microphones, and possibly additional people in the sound crew. Wild sound is independent of camera operation and it has its own requirements. Dubbing in the dialogue after the picture has been edited is called post-dubbing. It is quite expensive and time consuming, as recording studios and additional talent cost must be paid.

Sound is edited in postproduction, but the original bidder must know, what sound is expected from production.

Because the production company usually bids for operations up to developing the negative and a work print, a top-quality laboratory must be used or problems will arise during postproduction.

Figure 3-4. Director/cameraman Andrew Costikyan using a 35-mm Arriflex with a zoom lens; the camera is mounted on a fluid head with a high-hat tripod.

(Courtesy Cinema Products Corp.)

Figure 3-3. Panavision 35-mm camera mounted on fluid head with a zoom lens.

Figure 3-5. A 16-mm CP-16 Reflex mounted on an O'Connor fluid head with legs.

Figure 3-6. An Eclair 16-mm camera setup with a prime lens and matte box.

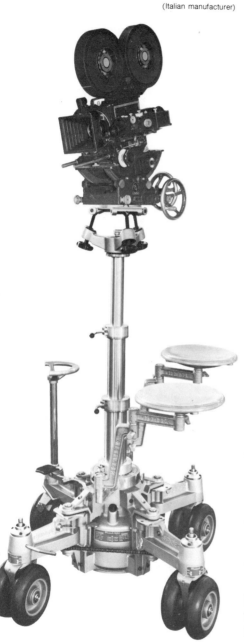

(Italian manufacturer)

Figure 3-7. A 16-mm camera with a lightweight geared head on an Elemack spyder dolly.

SELECTING THE PRODUCTION COMPANY

When the bids have all been received, they are carefully checked: the director's fee, days of shooting, weather-day charge, and markup are compared. If one estimate is extremely high, it can be discarded; or, if this bid comes from the preferred company, it can be contacted to make sure it had the right information. The very low bid can be handled in the same manner. It is extremely important that everyone understand the ingredients of the proposed commercials. Unauthorized charges after the completion of production can create a major billing problem.

The assignment of a spot to a production company is a major expenditure and is generally handled by the business department; the selection of the company is usually a group decision. The producer generally has a suggestion, but in most advertising agencies the creative director has the strongest voice; the concept must be produced and the concept is part of the creative department. A purchase order from the advertising agency followed by the initial payment to the production company starts the production wheels turning.

THE PREPRODUCTION MEETING

After the production job is awarded, it is necessary to meet with the people who are going to be directly involved in production. This preproduction meeting is usually be attended by the agency's writer or creative director, art director, and producer, and by the studio's director, production manager, and production assistant.

An agenda is prepared with agency comments regarding each part of the agenda. Points to be covered in a preproduction meeting include the following:

1. Objectives
2. Casting
3. Wardrobe
4. Sets
5. Locations
6. Props
7. Logistics
8. Schedule
9. Music

Some efficiency experts have determined that every hour of preproduction saves two hours of actual production, but some production factors cannot be foreseen. For example, there was the time in Bakersfield, California, when we were ready to shoot and the cameraman's exposure meter kept reading at progressively lower light levels. The cloudless sky above us added to the puzzle until a local bystander advised us we were in an area of total eclipse, and it had started.

On another occasion we were ready to do a power-tool demonstration for a national commercial. At the last minute, the client decided to supply the demonstrator, one of its sales managers. There was a sigh of relief when he appeared on the set, for he was a handsome, rugged-looking individual who was extremely articulate. As we lined up for the opening shot—a "head shot tilt down" to an extreme closeup of the hand sawing—our cameraman saw a problem. Our demonstrator did not have an index finger.

"Lost it in a little accident a few years ago," he cheeerfully informed us. The job was completed without any tilts to hand closeups; we cut to another person's hands for the closeups and hid our star's hands in the long shots.

These incidents indicate the kinds of problems that can arise on a set; the more extensive the preproduction, the better the agency can work through these problems and realize the concept.

Objectives

The objectives discussed in a preproduction meeting are mainly visual. The visual approach to a commercial must be understood clearly by the director, for it determines equipment, cameraman, lights, and props. This discussion might include the use of extreme-wide-angle lenses that distort and put the viewer close to the subject; use of lenses of a very long focal length, giving all the photography a compressed look with selective focus; use of moving cameras, zoom lenses, or hand-held cameras; use of low-level lighting to emphasize middletone gray and shadows; use of high-key lighting to give a brighter look to the subject; use of soft lights; control of image quality through camera work and laboratory processing to achieve high or lcw color saturation, high or low contrast, or grain.

Sound objectives should be completely covered, as they too can be handled in many ways: wireless microphones, shotgun (one-directional) mikes, pocket recorders, playback, dubbing. An editor can help make decisions about sound because post-production is heavily involved with sound. Marketing objectives may receive only brief mention, but every aspect of the production objectives should be fully discussed and agreed upon in this meeting.

Casting

Preproduction is the time to decide on casting. A date for the casting session should be set; a decision on whether to videotape the auditions must also be made. This taping adds expense, but being able to review the audition is an excellent idea. Perhaps the need may arise for a call-back session for final selection and videotaping. Many SAG rules concern auditions, and therefore casting services are frequently used to arrange auditions.

"Name" talent to be used in a commercial is usually contracted by the agency because of legal requirements and product association. These contracts not only stipulate money and time but also clarify arrangements for other advertising, promotion, even attendance at sales meetings. In this case, the director should be informed of the arrangements. Guild actors can only work on commercials for agencies and production companies that are signatories to the union agreement, which specifies that session fees be paid by the production company and all use and reuse payments be paid by the agency. The agreement also fines both agency and studio for late payments, long auditions, failure to fill out forms, or use of nonunion talent. If the spot does not air immedi-

ately, the agency must pay a holding fee to the talent.

We were once set to shoot a Reynolds Aluminum commercial showing an aluminum powerboat pulling a beautiful water skier through a series of intricate maneuvers. The helicopter was scheduled and the camera mount was installed; the forecast called for an hour of sun at 11:00 A.M. At the casting session on the previous day, all auditioners were questioned at length regarding their skiing ability; the chosen performer had assured us that she was "born on water." At the moment of truth, just as everyone was briefed and the clock was running at $2,000 an hour, she confided in me, "I hope you get this on the first take because I've never done it before." Our beautiful assistant director doubled for her and the shot was made.

Casting can be a commercial's single most important ingredient. The above incident illustrates the importance of not only casting but auditioning special talent. The casting session can take place anywhere that is convenient—at an independent casting office, at the agency, or at the production studio. It is very important to have the director at the final casting session. Some actors give terrific auditions but have trouble in front of cameras; others can intimidate clients at a session; still others may look great but have poor voice quality; and some have trouble memorizing their lines. I once directed a commercial in which the presenter worked from "idiot cards" (cue cards). His opening line, read directly from the cards, was, "Hi there, I'm (announcer's name) and I'm here to talk to you about stomach acid.'' The poor guy couldn't even ad-lib his own name; he had been cast by the agency. From experience, a good director anticipates such problems.

The SAG and AFTRA refer to casting sessions as auditions, and their standard commercials contract spells out rules and regulations. The following is a simplified interpretation of some of the most important:

1. An audition must be scheduled.
2. Reports of auditions must be made to the guild office.
3. The first hour of the audition is free; after that, the actor must be paid.
4. A first and second audition are permitted with the same rules applying.
5. A third audition must be paid.
6. A fourth and any subsequent audition must be paid at a premium rate; pension and welfare payments also apply.
7. Cue cards or their equivalent (tele-prompter) must be supplied when videotaping a speaking part.
8. If memorization is required, an additional fee must be paid.
9. Performers must be provided with scripts or storyboards at the time of audition sign-in.
10. Adequate seating must be provided.
11. Mass auditions (commonly referred to as ''cattle calls'') are prohibited.
12. Improvisation or ad libbing during the audition requires an additional payment.
13. Complete information regarding the role must be given if any unusual activity is required.

It is imperative to check with all performers to see if they are currently appearing on any competitive commercials. The casting agent or the individual performer should be aware of any commercials that might conflict with the product or company for which they are auditioning. In recent years the product has become more of an issue than the company; it is now legally permissible, for instance, to do a commercial for a Zenith radio and one for an RCA television set. This may nonetheless appear to be a conflict to the agencies and companies involved, however.

An incident of casting conflict occurred in a series of bank commercials that I directed. The featured spokesman assured us that there was no conflict in his speaking for a large Detroit bank; he had no other bank commercials in the area. Five commercials were produced before we found that our spokesman was currently featured on a commercial for the Detroit Savings and Loan Association. A savings and loan company is certainly not a bank; but the product, savings, is identical. His agent resolved the problem by contacting both agencies and making an acceptable agreement. We were all fortunate because the savings and loan association soon dropped its commercial.

Many areas of conflict are not easily defined. Is an airline principal in conflict if she is also featured in an railroad commercial? What about a beer commercial and a dietary aid, or beer and milk? How broad are the classifications? A decision can only be made if everyone at the casting session is aware of all the performer's current commercials and of all the agencies that are paying a holding fee.

Wardrobe

At the preproduction meeting, wardrobe for the performing talent should be discussed in detail; sketches are made available in special circumstances. Talent brings its own wardrobe to many commercials, but special costuming must be the responsibility of the production company and is covered in its bid.

A wardrobe check should be made before the day of shooting. If the talent is paid union scale, a charge is made for this fitting or check.

Sets

A date should be set for submission of set sketches. A studio set designer or art director is usually brought in; sometimes the agency has a preference for a set designer. The set designer not only makes set sketches but also supervises the construction and propping of the sets. On location, the art director is responsible for redressing.

A prelight day is a good idea on many productions: lights can be rigged with a minimum crew, sets can be dressed, and props can be set so everything is ready by shooting day. The costs of overtime with a full crew and actors are very high, so a prelight day could save much money.

Locations

Using a storyboard as a reference, the principals thoroughly discuss location requirements. Polaroid photographs are generally taken of potential locations for client approval. Frequently, these photos are taken as part of the production company's sales effort, to show its interest in the job. A date must be set for a physical check of locations.

In many states and in some large cities, a motion-picture and television office will help locate and clear locations. If this is not available, I have found that the local chamber of commerce is usually very helpful.

The agency is usually concerned with a location's appearance. In addition, the production company must also consider electric power, clearances, parking, travel time, catering, and a multitude of other details.

Props

It is important to make a detailed prop list so responsibility is allotted to the proper parties. Set props and location props are usually the production company's responsibility. Clients supply their own products, but they must realize the merchandise's photographic requirements. Beer commercials need cases of the product and might also require special labels; simplified labels are usually made of all packaging. Agencies or clients must approve all TV-color-corrected labels well in advance of shooting.

Logistics

Call times—the times that actors and crew are told to report for work—are not identical. On a studio shoot it is not unusual to have an early call for makeup and talent, then camera crew and stagehands, then clients. On a location shoot everyone has an early call so traveling time does not affect the time available at location. Moving props, crew, talent, equipment, and clients from one location to another is an important part of production planning. Having lunch can be a problem in logistics. With union crews, five hours is the maximum time allowed between meals. It is sometimes a smart production move to cater a buffet breakfast so the director can have five straight hours of shooting. Most location lunches and dinners are catered to save time. A small nonunion crew offers a financial advantage to the production company, as it has no such rules. Everything in preplanning is aimed at making the shooting day a good, efficient experience by having all needed elements readily available.

Schedule

In matters of schedule, the delivery date must be the first consideration. After this is established, the other parts of the schedule are figured backwards from this date. (Usually this proves that the job should have started last week.) One month is an approximate production time for completing a film commercial. A typical production schedule is the following:

Preproduction—7 working days
   Location search and clearing
   Set sketches and construction
   Casting and wardrobe
Production—3 working days
   Prelight
   Shooting (2-day schedule)
   Laboratory
   Sound transfers
Postproduction—10 working days
   Editing
   Screenings
   Recordings and mixing
   Opticals
   Composite prints

The total of twenty working days can be shortened by about five days if videotape finishing is used. Laboratory photographic work is much more time consuming than electronic processing, especially in opticals and composite prints.

The support technicians must also be scheduled. Makeup and hairdressing are a usual requirement; and, if food is to be prepared for photography, a home economist, stoves, ovens, and hot plates might be necessary. Drivers for vehicles (teamster-union members in some areas), caterers, dressing rooms, toilet facilities, and any other services must be supplied by the production company. Shooting day is D day, and all contingencies must be covered.

Music

If music is to be composed especially for the picture, the director and composer might discuss the handling of the visuals. Often the music is prerecorded and played during shooting for timing or mouthing of words. This is referred to as a playback track and can be produced by the agency, but it must be ready before the shooting day. A playback track can be voice only, voice and piano, or a full finished track with an orchestra and singers. This track is synchronized with the picture during postproduction editing. When the preproduction meeting has been completed, everyone should understand what must be done before photography can begin. The shooting day becomes the most important deadline to be met. Although the production company has the brunt of this responsibility, production is at all times a cooperative project with the advertising agency.

CHAPTER

FILM PRODUCTION

Production is the culmination of all the time and effort spent in preproduction. The motion-picture industry has been around for half a century, and motion-picture production is very well organized (perhaps overorganized), with well-established unions having jurisdiction over most workers in the industry. Since the greatest percentage of television commercials is made by motion-picture crews, their organizations dominate production. As new people enter the commercial business, the control of the traditional unions is diluted; it is possible to produce nonunion. There are many excellent nonunion companies all over the country, but to explain the working of a production crew I will use the union breakdown of job classification (Figure 4-1). In nonunion production, crews are smaller because there is a great deal of overlap in job functions.

There are three absolutely essential roles in commercial production: a client (the advertising agency), someone in charge (the director), and someone shooting the pictures (the cameraman). Everyone else involved in production is in a support position.

One such support occupation at the studio is the production manager or producer, who takes care of business details, hires free-lancers, keeps the crew up to date on budgets, sets up schedules, and tries to juggle personnel to keep everyone happy when the company has more than one crew in production.

THE PRODUCTION CREW

The production manager of the production company, or the studio producer, usually assembles the production crew after a thorough discussion with the director and agency producer. It generally breaks down into the following classifications:

1. Director
2. Assistant director
3. Cameraman
4. Assistant cameraman
5. Production assistants
6. Art director and stylist
7. Gaffer and electricians
8. Key grip and grips
9. Sound crew
10. Script clerk (continuity clerk)
11. Specialists

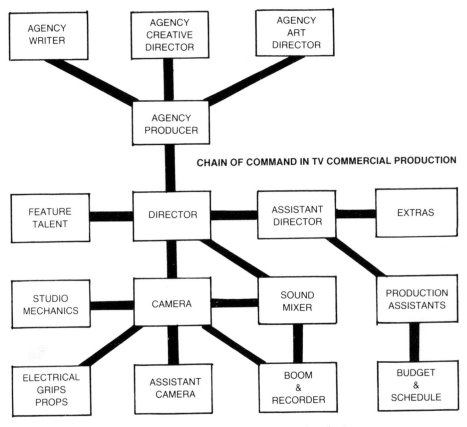

CHAIN OF COMMAND IN TV COMMERCIAL PRODUCTION

Figure 4-1. A film-production organization chart.

This is the type of film crew found in major film centers such as New York, Chicago, Los Angeles, Dallas, Miami, Ft. Lauderdale, Detroit, and others. Many companies produce commercials without such a staff, but some people are doing more than one job; all the above functions must be performed (Figure 4-2).

Director

The most important member of the crew, and the prime talent that the production company sells the agency, is the director. Originally, directors received their training in motion pictures. In the 1950s, a motion-picture background was essential for the making of film commercials; live commercials remained the domain of TV technicians and engineers. The film director worked on the floor, and the TV director worked from a booth. After videotape replaced live commercials, TV directors continued in this area. In the 1960s, TV and motion-picture techniques started mixing, and the Radio and Television Directors Guild

(RTDG) merged with the Directors Guild of America (DGA).

The Directors Guild publishes a pamphlet that attempts to explain the director's duties. They explain:

Many metaphors have been applied aptly to the role of the director—the captain and coach of the team; the architect and builder of the structure; the father, or mother, as the case may be, of the offspring.

It is not possible briefly to set down all that a director does. But in simple terms, the director has sole charge and makes final artistic judgments during three basic phases of making motion pictures and television productions on film, tape, or live.

In *preproduction*, the director makes decisions on final script, casting, sets, costumes, props, effects, locations, budgets, and schedule.

In *production*, the director not only directs the actors but places the cameras and chooses the lenses and otherwise composes the scenes and the people to tell a story, whether for a feature film, a television production, or the evening news. All the while the director exercises full responsibilities of a "captain" commanding a complex group of talented persons, the production company.

In *postproduction*, the director oversees the editing, dubbing, scoring, and other finishing processes that bring a film up to preview or a television show up to broadcast. (from *The First 45 Years*, Directors Guild of America, Hollywood, California, 1980).

(Courtesy Gootson-Oakes-Schumacher Productions, Inc)

Figure 4-2. A TV commercial in production. Director, cameraman, and assistant cameraman are on the crane, client supervisors are observing.

Although most TV-commercial directors belong to the DGA, they have relinquished to the advetising agency many of their traditional controls, including casting, script approval, and editorial supervision. Because the agency is both author and sponsor of the production, this is not surprising.

In the 1970s, some advertising-agency art directors began directing commercials because of their experience directing illustration photography. Still photographers also took up the motion-picture camera and became both photographers and directors of TV commercials. Today there are very few, if any, well-known television-commercial directors who were exclusively motion-picture directors; most of the current ones came from advertising agencies or were television directors. The directors of long films such as theatrical features, TV program material, and industrial documentaries still get their training in the motion picture and television industries.

The director of television commercials must think like a writer, see like an art director, handle people like a personnel manager, and have the personality to keep on an even keel when the going is rough. And somewhere there must be a good businessman or everything could be lost. These qualities combined in one person mark a rare creature and are responsible for the director's star status.

Assistant Director

The assistant director is more than the name implies. He or she generally assists the director by doing the non-creative work that is the director's responsibility. By job description the assistant director organizes pre-production, including assembling the crew, securing equipment, breaking down the script, preparing shooting schedule, assisting the director during production with respect to on-set details, coordinating crew and cast activities, and facilitating the flow of production activities. In some cases the assistant director secures cast contracts and supervises background action. Call times, weather reports, and location clearances are also the assistant director's responsibility. In many so-called boutique operations (small production companies that do specialized work) the job of assistant director is performed by many production assistants. The DGA claims assistant directors as part of its organization; non-signatory companies may do anything they wish to fill this function.

Cameraman

The cameraman is almost as important as the director. The commercial's "look" is the cameraman's responsibility, in conjunction with the director's desires. This is why, in most cases, the cameraman is selected by the director. In some circumstances the agency asks for a cameraman because of previous work or because it feels a particular commercial is a cameraman's, rather than a director's, spot. There is a trend for cameramen to add direction to their work, and many directors become cameramen as they learn the photographic aspects of the work. The director/cameraman combination works very well in commercial production, as it minimizes communication problems. This combination is also possible because of the production company's lessened workload: many of the director's traditional responsibilities are handled by the advertising agency. Casting, editing, and writing are no longer the sole duties of the production studio and its director.

Assistant Cameraman

The assistant cameraman is directly responsible to the cameraman and has a very important job. In England the assistant cameraman is called the focus puller, because it is his responsibility to keep objects in focus for the cameraman by manipulating the lenses during shooting. In addition, the assistant cameraman checks the equipment, loads film, carries equipment, takes exposure readings, keeps an accurate log sheet, and does anything else that the cameraman needs. The team of cameraman and assistant is very important, and a good combination can make life easier for the director.

Production Assistants

There may be many production assistants on a crew. They work for either the production manager or studio producer and do anything necessary—search for locations, procure props, wardrobe, permits, and "gofer" whatever is needed. The broadness of the term indicates the variety of work that they might do, particularly in non-union operations. This is usually a foot-in-the-door job: most production assistants hope to become assistant directors.

Art Director and Stylist

The art director of a television commercial works closely with the director and usually designs and supervises set construction and specifies and supervises prop placement. On location, the art director might redress and add new elements. This is a very creative position, so it is not unusual for the art director to work closely with the advertising agency.

On some crews this function is performed by a stylist. This title originated in the photo-illustration studios. The stylist must have excellent taste and is frequently used as an interior decorator. He or she is not usually an artist, but if the storyboard has been rendered with a lot of detail, a stylist might be perfect for the commercial. Either the art director or stylist must be responsible for the overall appearance of the set or location.

Gaffer and Electricians

The gaffer, or head electrician, does no physical labor on big lighting setups, but supervises the electricians in the placing of lights and the hooking up of cables. Many small crews do not use this title. Electricians hook up electricity, move lights, run electrical generators, and do anything the gaffer tells them to do.

Key Grip and Grips

As in the previous classification, this title reflects big-production nomenclature. In New York and Los Angeles the people who rig cameras for special setups, push dollies, set cutters and gobos (light blockers), and handle properties are called grips. In smaller productions and in other regions, this work is performed by the general studio mechanics or stagehands. Because a great deal of production is done in New York and Los Angeles, grip is still used for this job.

Sound Crew

When shooting synchronous sound, the sound crew is on set throughout filming. Depending on the sound's complexity and union requirements, the size of the sound crew varies from one to four people. The floor mixer is in charge and controls quality by monitoring while recording. The boomman moves the microphone on a boom (movable beam) for optimum pickup. The recorder records the sound. A cableman might be needed if there are a number of microphones and many lines and cables. In a typical commercial production it is very unusual to have more than two people, the mixer/recorder and the boomman, in a sound crew.

Script Clerk (Continuity Clerk)

Whenever sync sound is shot, a professional script clerk should be on the crew. A properly kept script indicates the preferred take (both picture and sound), a second choice, and the portion of the script that each take covers (Figure 4-3). In addition, the script clerk times all segments of the script as they are shot, makes sure the dialogue is accurate, keeps track of wardrobe changes, advises the director on matching action on cuts, makes notes on the shooting script for the editor's information, and sometimes serves as a general production assis-

tant. All the script clerk's notations appear on a copy of the script or shot list and expedite postproduction.

Specialists

These are not regular crew members but people who might be required for special jobs.

Home economist: One is needed for photographic food preparation.

Wardrobe: A specialist is needed to make alterations and handle costumes.

Makeup and hairdressers: On cosmetic commercials, this is a must; most commercials use makeup personnel—some use hairdressers.

Choreographer: If there is any dancing or graceful moves required, this helps.

Drivers: The teamster's union supplies drivers for all vehicles, particularly in New York and Los Angeles; small production units and nonunion companies drive their own.

Stunt people: Stunt work is not for amateurs. The New York or Los Angeles stuntmen organizations should be contacted if dangerous stunts are required.

AGENCY PRODUCER AND DIRECTOR

One of the most important ingredients in producing a successful commercial is a good rapport between the agency supervisor, usually called the producer, and the director. The producer is generally part of the production group, but could be a creative representative or even an account person. He or she must be an excellent handler of people. During shooting, it

PRODUCTION: #81-035   FORD
DIRECTOR: JON
CAMERAMAN: JOHN
SCRIPT SUPERVISOR: MARY

DATE: 7/7/81   PAGE: 1
1st SHOT: 10:30
LUNCH:
1st PM SHOT:
WRAP CALLED:

SC.#	ACTION	TK	SND	TIME	REMARKS	ROLL
1	EXT. CAR - DAY		1	:06	—	CR1-SR1
	START WIDE AND		2	:06	BAD TILT	
	ZOOM IN ON ROSE		3	.06½	LONG	
	(BEHIND WHEEL) THEN		4	:06	MIC	
	PAN UP TO BILL.		5	:07	DOOR	
	BILL SAYS "BEAUTFUL"		6	INC	—	
			7	INC	MIC	
			8	:05½	NG - CMA	
			⑨	:06	OK	
			10	:06	LATE ZOOM	
	N.B. TOTAL TIMING		11	.06	NG SND	
	TO :28½		12	:06	FLUB	
			13	:06	SHIRT BAD	
			14	:06	?	
			15	:07	LONG	
			⑯	:06	OK	
		X	⑰	.06	VERY GOOD	
1A	ALTERNATE ON 1		18	:06	BAD SOUND	
	START TIGHT ON ROSE		19	.06	MIC	
	PULL BACK TO		⑳	:06	GOOD	
	FULL SHOT - BILL		21	:06	BAD MOVE	
	SAYS "BEAUTIFUL"		22	:06½	LONG	
		X	㉓	:06	OK-BEST	
2	CU - ROSE REACTS		24	:08	TOO LONG	
	AND SAYS TO CAMERA		25	:07+	NOT LIVELY	
	" I NEVER THOUGHT		26	:07+	NG SOUND	
	HE'D NOTICE etc... "		㉗	:07+	OK -SOUND?	
	MAX :7½		㉘	:07	GOOD	
			29	.07+	FLUB	
			30	:07	NG - CMA	
		X	㉛	:07+	NICE	
		X	㉜	:07	BEST	

Figure 4-3. Script notes as kept by the script clerk for the editor.

is customary to have many interested agency people on the set. If all of them try to give suggestions to the director, the shoot grows expensive and confusing. The director must be able to work through one person who can give a single voice to the many comments raised by bystanders. Without an effective agency supervisor, the director might have more problems directing the people behind the camera than those in front of it.

When all is said and done, the agency often chooses a production studio on the strength of the director's talent, so it is important for the agency supervisor to take advantage of it. The director tends to be more objective, since he or she has not been deeply involved in the weeks of planning at the outset of the project and can make excellent contributions to enhance or "plus" the original script. While giving the director support, the producer must keep the requirements of the script and storyboard in sight. This continuous balancing act is one of the most important and difficult parts of broadcast production.

The director, in fact and by tradition, is the boss of the crew and has leadership on the set. This makes film production an extremely efficient operation. When the director loses control, chaos results. A director who agrees to many points of view may be a joy to work with on the set, but the finished production may well be a lifeless compromise.

Because the director has not lived with a commercial through all of its planning stages, the preproduction meeting must completely inform him

or her. When the shooting day arrives, the producer must keep the director informed of any changes. A director who has been shooting commercials for years becomes very accustomed to the presence of the agency supervisor and other client representatives. While directing a group of commercials in Chicago for a Texas ad agency, I received a call from the producer on the morning of the shoot. He could not make it and wanted me to proceed without him. My first reaction was one of relief, but on the second setup I realized there was no one to whom I could raise a question, no one with whom I could argue.

A young J. Walter Thompson producer happened to be in our studio at the time. When he found out that the Texas producer was absent, he offered to substitute in spite of the fact that he knew nothing about the client and was not connected with the Texas agency. I accepted his offer and we had a fine shooting day; he questioned setups and asked why I was doing each scene in that particular way. The spots were approved by the agency at the first cut. The Texas producer received many compliments, and the J. Walter Thompson producer received my thanks.

The performing talent is very dependent on the director for instructions in all acting details and for approval. The cameraman is continually checking with the director for camera position, lenses, camera movement, lighting, and timing. Generally the director rehearses the complete scene in front of the cameras before it is filmed. At this time the lighting is refined and the camera movements polished. This is also the time for the producer to inform the director of any last-minute agency comments. Relighting and changing camera positions after a first take are expensive and irritating to everyone. When the director and the producer work well together, the shooting day is a very pleasant experience for all.

CAMERA AND SOUND

As the shooting day approaches, two important determinations must still be made: the cameraman and soundman must be hired. Some cameramen—especially when they are director-cameramen—are permanent employees of the production companies, but generally this is a freelance specialty. Sound is always hired on a per-job basis.

The camerman, sometimes referred to as the photographer, is usually selected because of the type of photography needed in the commercial. Most cameramen feel that they are excellent at all types of work, but directors and producers probably disagree with them. In my own opinion, food photography is definitely a specialty; not everyone can do fashion photography; automobile work in the studio (frequently called "sheet-iron work") has a technique all of its own; and very few have the feelings for unique-viewpoint camerawork (see Chapter 2, page 31). A preparation (prep) day should be scheduled for the cameraman to check on equipment and lights. If the production staff has ordered the equipment, the prep day can be used as a prelight day.

Before contracting for sound, all sound requirements must be considered. Sound companies supply personnel and the latest in recording and transfer equipment. Many times, individual sound people are hired and equipment is rented separately. This decision might be made because of a personal preference for a particular floor mixer, or perhaps a budget consideration. Services are usually more expensive than individuals.

Photography and Lighting

The cameraman is responsible for the commercial's photography; the duties of a motion-picture director of photography and camera operator are usually combined in the television-commercial camerman. On occasions when the director is the cameraman, it is sometimes wise to have a separate camera operator. The photography of a commercial incorporates not only film, lenses, filters, focus, exposure, mechanical operation, and camera, but also the intangibles of composition, camera movement, and the total look of the pictures. This look depends heavily on lighting.

It is impossible to make an exact science of this phase of production because photography and lighting standards change constantly in response to advertising trends. Also, the relationship between the cameraman and the director is a very personal one, often based on long and successful association; what I relate about this important phase of production is personal.

When I entered the television-commercial field in the early 1950s, I was a director trying to take agency radio writers' copy one step further into the dimension of pictures. Since we were going to make motion pictures of these commercials, the first order of business was a phone call to the International Alliance of Theatrical and Stage Employees (IATSE), the union for motion-picture cameramen, to ask it to send us its best available cameraman for a job.

The union sent Loren Tutell. He was an excellent man who had operated for many of the great directors of photography during the 1930s and '40s. He brought his vast experience in black-and-white feature production to our studio. I set up the shot, blocked the action, picked the viewpoint, and gave him instructions about what I wanted. He photographed it. This is still the basic director-cameraman relationship.

Once the scene was rehearsed he had a very definite pattern of lighting—a key light for the feature subject, special lights for separation and for lighting the walls, small spotlights for kicks and accents, soft floor lights for fill. There was never a mike-boom shadow on the set, and he knew how to light for camera and performer movement. The small closeups, however, were not important to Tutell; he referred to them as insert shots to be made when the real work was finished (Figure 4-4). Loren Tutell's techniques, which evolved from the idealism of theatrical films, could make a forty-year-old woman look like a teenage beauty. Standard advertising photography leaned more to realism: a housewife holding up a box of detergent.

Television is not wide-screen motion

Figure 4-4. A director/cameraman shooting an insert with a 35-mm Panavision camera.

pictures, and as time went on, the size of the television picture seemed to demand a greater concern for those inserts. By the time color arrived, closeups became the name of the game on the TV tube. Soon advertising-agency art directors were requesting that a still-illustration photographer be on the set for closeups. Print illustrations were used as a guide for TV commercials, and motion-picture photographers duplicated the effects of the strobe lights, bounce lights, and long exposures that were possible in still photos. Many still photographers learned motion-picture techniques, and motion-picture photographers learned advertising lighting.

There are different colors of basic light in the everyday world. A motion-picture cameraman duplicates or supplements this light. Indoor light is yellow and outdoor light is quite blue;

look at a burning indoor bulb next to a window and you will see the difference. The temperature of light varies with its color. Incandescent light is approximately 3,200 degrees Kelvin and outdoor light is about 5,400 degrees Kelvin. To match these colors a variety of lamps is needed. For years, arc lights were used to supplement outdoor lighting, but a new family of lamps and fixtures called HMI lights seems to be replacing them. Other types of cool (5,400°K) lights are also being used. Incandescent lamps have generally remained the same through the years (Figures 4-5 through 4-7).

The picture area of television is also a consideration in television photography. Television's aspect ratio—the height of the picture compared to its width—is 3:4. Although this is the approximate proportion of the motion-picture frame, many allowances must be made for the area of the picture that is lost in transmission and reception. This allowance must be made during filming and a TV-viewing glass is manufactured that indicates the TV

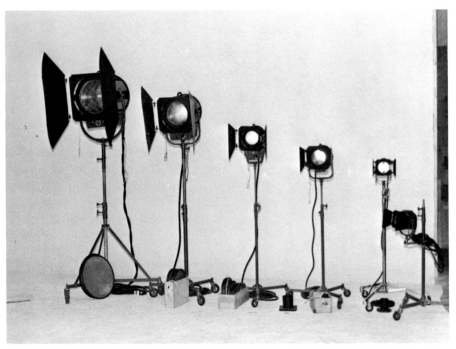

(Courtesy RAH Lighting, Inc.)

Figure 4-5. An assortment of standard studio spotlights with accessory screening material. Wattages are from 150 to 5,000. *Left to right*: the popular names are senior, baby senior, baby junior, baby, and inkie.

cutoff. The ground glass fits into the camera and shows the "safe" areas as the scene is viewed. Since the complete frame is exposed and printed, a reminder of the area that might be lost in transmission is indicated any time the picture is viewed.

There is no definite pattern to good television lighting and composition; each scene is composed and lit to the best of the cameraman's ability. In the standard thirty-second commercial, every scene is extremely important; each must be able to withstand the criticism of ad agency, client, and viewer.

Figure 4-7. HMI lights with their ballasts, which convert the standard AC to DC. Normally matching daylight color, they can be converted for studio use. *Left to right*: 4,000 watts, 2,500 watts, 1,200 watts.

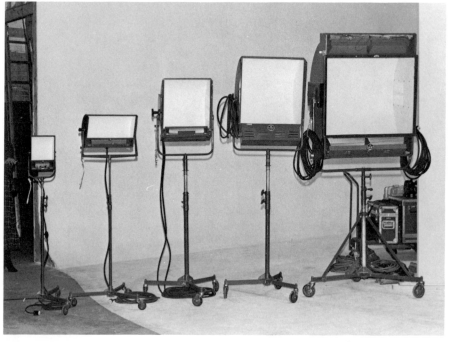

(Courtesy RAH Lighting, Inc.)

Figure 4-6. Studio soft lights throw a very diffused illumination. *Left to right*: 1,000 watts, 2,000 watts, 2,000 watts, 4,000 watts, 8,000 watts.

(Courtesy RAH Lighting, Inc.)

Sound

Completing the sound track is usually a postproduction function. When a voice-over track with music is required, it is likely that the production company will have nothing to do with it; it will only be concerned with the visuals. The advertising agency generally produces this track by dealing directly with the voice talent and the music company and then supervising the recording. Synchronous sound is part of production, and the production company must deliver high-quality sound. Most synchronous sound consists of the on-camera performers' speech, and there are a number of recording methods available.

The first requirement in shooting synchronous sound is equipment. The camera runs at exactly twenty-four frames per second, and the tape recorder must be able to record at that exact speed (Figure 4-8). The camera usually has a motor controlled by a crystal generator, and the recorder has a reference pulse placed on it to ensure accurate speed.

The next problem is microphoning the sound (Figures 4-9 and 4-10). The traditional—and best—method of picking up the sound from a performer is to fasten a microphone to the end of a boom; the boomman keeps the mike as close as possible to the speaker but out of camera range. Properly han-

Figure 4-8. The Nagra tape recorder in use on location.

dled, this method produces the highest-quality sound because the mike is in the open in front of the performer. Unfortunately, this type of pickup also collects ambient (surrounding) sound and poses lighting problems for the cameraman.

A small button microphone that is placed very close to a speaker's mouth reduces the background noise and simplifies boom manipulation and lighting problems (Figure 4-11). These small microphones are usually hung

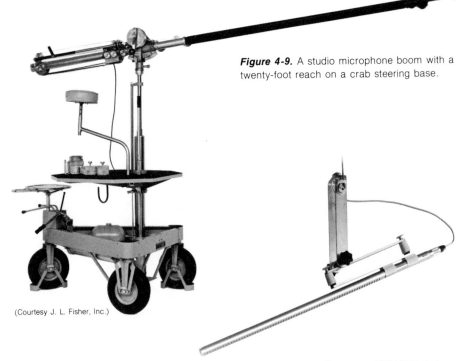

Figure 4-9. A studio microphone boom with a twenty-foot reach on a crab steering base.

(Courtesy J. L. Fisher, Inc.)

Figure 4-10. The Sennheiser MKH 805 shotgun microphone, a unidirectional mike with shock mount to isolate it from vibration.

around the actor's neck, often hidden from view. Some have small clips to attach to wearing apparel. Even though they are placed below the speaker's chin, these microphones give good results. The problem is that they are usually connected to the recorder by a wire, and this limits movement somewhat and makes picture-cropping critical. Under ideal conditions, the wire can be replaced by a very small radio transmitter about the size of a cigarette pack. The transmitter can be hidden on the performer, and the signals can be picked up by a small receiver at the recorder. Unfortunately, this wireless system sometimes picks up interference. A good sound man is always prepared with options (Figure 4-12). Specific microphones are designed for optimum sound pickup in particular areas.

Some cameras are used to record both picture and sound on one piece of film; these are referred to as single system. When sound is recorded on a piece of equipment separate from the camera, the procedure is referred to as double system. All television commercials use the double system because of its superior quality. Because the double system means separate picture and sound recordings, it is imperative that they always be kept in perfect sync. According to industry standards, more than a one-frame variation between picture and sound track is not acceptable.

In emergencies, dialogue can be made after the commercial has been completed. This method may be necessary because the location sound was unintelligible or had too much extraneous noise. This procedure is referred to as looping (also called click tracking or postdubbing) and is very common in European productions, which tend not to be concerned about sound quality while shooting. In looping the start of a scene is spliced to the end of the same scene, forming a circle or loop. This scene can then be projected continuously on a screen while the voice talent watches and tries to synchronize voices to lip

(Courtesy Sony Corp.)

Figure 4-11. A small button or tie-tack microphone.

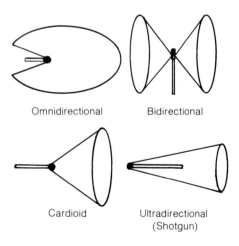

Omnidirectional   Bidirectional

Cardioid   Ultradirectional
(Shotgun)

Figure 4-12. Microphone recording patterns.

movements. The voices are then recorded and matched with the picture.

The computer has now taken over part of the postdubbing operation with a system called automatic dialogue replacement (ADR). It is no longer necessary to loop the film because the computer controls both the projector and the tape recorder and keeps repeating the scene until it is successfully dubbed.

The opposite technique is to prerecord the dialogue and photograph the commercial to the playback. Synchronous equipment must be used for both camera and sound. The prerecorded sound is played on the set with a recorded countdown before the first word. The actors hear 1, 2, 3, and, on beat, they start. After this point, the rhythm of the voice or music keeps them in sync. Most musical production is prerecorded so the best recording can be played over and over while the scene is photographed from many angles. A big musical scene could be shot from a dozen camera positions, and a dozen good sound takes would be impossible. With the playback, only the picture needs to be edited.

Nonsynchronous or wild sound is recorded separately. Most sound effects are made in this manner. This permits the changing of camera speeds for special effects and the use of small, easy-to-handle cameras that are noisy. Announcer (voice-over) tracks are usually made in a recording studio, but they can also be made wild on the sound stage if schedule or budget dictates.

SHOOTING DAY

The first on-set activity of the shooting day is setting up the camera. A 35-mm camera is usually broken down into a number of cases to withstand shipment; a 35-mm Panavision comes in as many as twelve cases. The assistant cameraman usually assembles the camera, constantly checking with the cameraman about type of lenses, mounts, viewers, magazines, film stock, and other accessories. The director, cameraman, and gaffer discuss lighting while the camera is readied, and other members of the crew scurry around putting final touches on the set and props.

The first setup is planned by the director and cameraman, and the agency producer is checked to make sure of the agency's approval. The cables for the lights are strung as the gaffer starts to rough-light the set. By this time the talent is ready for a run-through. Makeup and hairdressing are frequently used on commercials, and the call time should be early enough for the talent to be ready when the crew is.

The run-through of the first scene indicates lighting problems to the cameraman and gaffer, and the sound department can determine its approach to microphoning. The cameraman might ask the gaffer for some lights to be trimmed: perhaps a cutter to be placed, a gobo to be set, a cucaloris to break up the background, a net or silk to cut down or diffuse a light (Figures 4-13 through 4-16). All these lighting refinements are typical of the professional film maker.

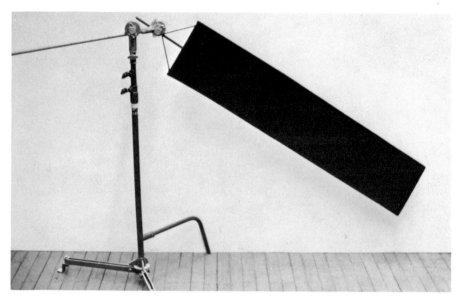

Figure 4-13. A cutter on a stand; it is used to reduce light in a selected area.

Figure 4-14. The standard gobo, used to reduce light on a scene.

Figure 4-15. Shooting on the stage using a cucaloris or "cookie" (upper left) to break up the light pattern.

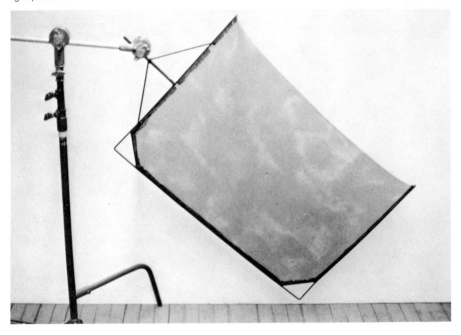

Figure 4-16. A net used in front of a light to balance and control its values.

The camera is usually mounted on a tripod, a dolly, or a crane, but it can also be hand held or mounted on a Steadicam-type mount that gives a very smooth move to a hand-held operation (Figures 4-17 and 4-18).

The camera is mounted either on a fluid head or, because of its size and weight, on a geared head. If the camera is to move smoothly during the take, it is sometimes necessary to lay tracks for the dolly (Figure 4-19). The cameraman or his assistant takes light readings with an exposure meter to check the amount and balance of light (Figure 4-20). They may even check the light color with a color meter. The cameraman then tells the director "Ready on camera." Sound indicates "Sound is OK." The assistant director notifies everyone to "Stand by," and the director might then say "OK, let's make it!"

For a sync take, the talent gets into position and they next hear, "Roll sound." The floor mixer looks at the recorder, makes sure it has settled down, and calls "Speed." The cameraman hits the camera switch and says "Sticks," and the assistant closes out the familiar clap sticks on the slate (Figure 4-21) after calling out the number of the sound take (and anything else he deems pertinent).

(Courtesy J. L. Fisher, Inc.)

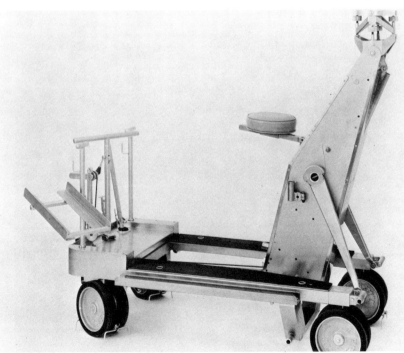

Figure 4-17. The popular Fisher camera dolly.

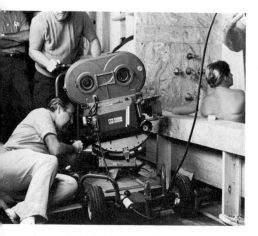

Figure 4-18. A 35-mm BNC Mitchell camera mounted on a geared head on a high hat on a Costikyan western dolly.

When the assistant cameraman has cleared the set, the director says "Action," and the scene continues until the director calls "Cut." Only the director should call "Cut," because no one else is sure what part of the scene will be used in the editing.

After the take, comments can be made to the director by crew and producer. The mixer might not like the sound and the cameraman might not like the composition. This could call for another take. Even if the take is acceptable, the producer might ask for another take because of interpretation.

(Courtesy Fortis and Fortis Advertising, Inc.)

Figure 4-19. Location shooting on a commercial with a 35-mm Panavision camera from a three-wheeled Fisher dolly on tracks.

Figure 4-20. The standard exposure meter used on most film production.

(Courtesy Victor Duncan, Inc.)

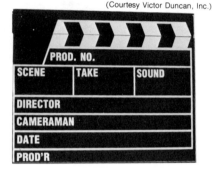

Figure 4-21. The Victor Duncan super slate.

It is very unusual to make only one take. Most scenes are repeated until there is one good take and an acceptable backup take as well. A script clerk notes the approved take and the elapsed time on each one to keep track of accumulated time for the director and to record information for the editor.

In television-commercial production, it is a good practice to print all takes. Work print is paid for by the foot, but by printing all takes the chance of scratching the original negative is minimized because the laboratory will not have to remove the NG (no good) negative from the printing roll. Another good reason is that many times a scene that appeared bad on the set looks good in the editing room. There is sometimes a happy accident that makes a good commercial.

As the shooting day continues, many written records are kept of the commercial's progress. The assistant cameraman and floor mixer keep an accurate take log that stays with their material throughout all processing. The master script kept by the clerk has complete notes and will be used by the editor for constant reference.

By union rules, meal breaks must be taken every five hours or a meal-penalty charge is added to the hourly rate. After the typical working day—either eight or ten hours—overtime charges are also made (Figure 4-22). Traveling to and from locations is figured as part of the working day. Whether shooting takes place in the studio or on location, the general procedures are usually the same. Problems with sound and lighting are greater when shooting on location, but the added time needed for location work is usually less than the cost of building sets and procuring props. (The decision about studio or location shooting has been made at the preproduction meeting.)

Even with a prelight day, the first hours of shooting seem confused. As the scenes are rehearsed and photographed, many questions come up, most of them relating to the amount of

Figure 4-22. A night location shoot; overtime can be costly.

time available for the scene. Acting out a scene always seems to take about 20 percent longer than reading it out loud. In addition to questions about timing, familiar questions asked about performers include, ''Why are they talking so loud?,'' ''Should they be smiling?,'' and ''Why can't they eat and talk at the same time?'' Ridiculous as these comments may sound, they illustrate the need for one person, the agency supervisor or producer, to function as the sole communicator with the director.

A recent addition to motion-picture equipment capability is the video-as-sist viewer and the videocassette tape recorder (VCR). The viewer is a small video pickup tube that is placed in the camera eyepiece and connected to a TV monitor on the set (Figure 4-23). A recorder can be connected so the takes can be rerun for review. This has become very common in network commercial production, and it removes much of the guesswork from production. All cameramen and directors are not pleased with this innovation, as it not only deprives them of some of their decision-making authority but also adds time to the production day. But only the camera viewpoint finds its way onto a projection screen—highlights, shadows, flares, and action that look bad from a casual chair on the set may present no problem when viewed through the camera—and the VCR enables all concerned to see the camera viewpoint.

Many times a scene is covered from many angles to make sure all involved individuals are happy. The practice became so overdone that in 1979 the SAG went on strike to win payments for each version photographed. There is also a cost element to be considered when excess versions are made: not only does the shooting time increase, but so does the amount of film stock. Every 1,000-foot roll of 35-mm film costs close to $1,000 when the price of raw stock, developing, and work print is totaled. The hourly rate for a crew is at least the same. It is very evident that the price goes up when a commercial is overproduced. This problem is best solved by the production company's notifying the agency producer and getting approval of the additional costs before proceeding. Unauthorized changes and additional billing are a prime reason for studio-agency disenchantment.

Each day after the completion of photography, the film is taken to the laboratory for processing. Labs will usually develop and print the "dailies" by the next morning. The director and producer screen the dailies as soon as practical to make sure that there are no problems. There are times when reshoots are needed because of camera scratches, picture flares, bad action, poor camera moves, or any other complications. After all the photogra-

phy has been completed, the daily work print is spliced in the proper sequence and screened with the sync sound. This type of screening can be projected on an interlock system (sound and projector running together), or it can be shown on an editor's console (see Chapter 5). Projection is always desirable because the large screen and picture quality permit proper inspection.

In television-commercial production, all dailies should be color- and density-timed at the laboratory so the quality of the photography can be analyzed at the screening. Many times unprofessional production companies show a poor work print with the ex-

Figure 4-23. Arri 35-3 with CPT video assist and base-mounted power supply; Fellini-style viewfinder attachment; 1,000-foot magazine; 20-120-mm Angenieux zoom lens with follow-focus and zoom motor drive.

cuse that the client is merely screening "one-light" work prints and that the color and density will be corrected in the final print. This excuse should not be accepted. Timed dailies might cost a bit more at the laboratory, but they are well worth it. It is best to know any problems while the commercial is still in production; reshoots are considerably cheaper when all of the production elements are assembled. The screening of dailies should reassure everyone on the production of the quality of the previous day's shooting.

Location shooting has its own set of problems (Figure 4-24). All the elements of studio production are involved, but the control element is lessened. Extraneous sound is always a problem on location, and a great amount of time is spent waiting for quiet periods to record sound. The electrical service on many locations does not suffice for lighting (Figure 4-25). This usually means renting a generator and hiring an operator to provide sufficient power. Parking for buses and cars must be considered,

Figure 4-24. An automobile commercial on location. Notice the HMI light in the foreground; it is used to supplement daylight and light up the car's interior.

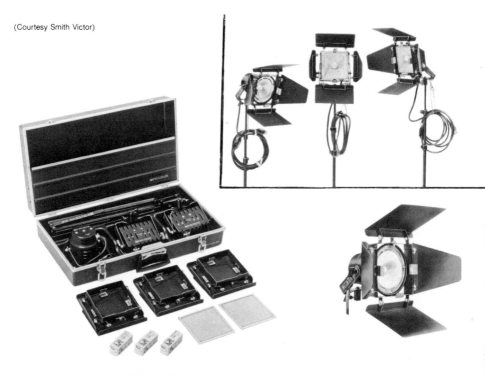

Figure 4-25. A very basic location lighting kit.

and permission or permits must be obtained. It might be necessary to rent trucks for props and equipment, hire teamsters to drive the trucks, or contact the police for crowd control. Toilet facilities for cast and crew could require the use of those portable rest rooms known as "honey wagons." Even lunch can be a problem.

There are many benefits to location work, especially capturing a "real-life" look; there is a lived-in look to a real house that can rarely be duplicated on the stage. Exterior work is nearly always a location project, although the back lots of many West Coast studios rent to TV-commercial production companies. The back lot of the large film studios falls under the controlled studio classification; it is also very expensive. The union rules of the rental studio apply to the renter; this means teamsters, department managers, and other staff people in addition to the regular production crew must be hired. Sometimes it is worth it.

Location in other countries is also a part of the TV-commercial production. Preproduction planning on this type of location work is imperative. Passports, vaccinations, custom clearances, tax clearances, and film processing must all be considered; but the most important element is to have someone on the crew who speaks the foreign language fluently. Whenever exterior shooting is planned, weather-day allowances should always be considered.

The production phase of making a TV commercial has always had a certain glamour connected to it. In my own experience, the glamour occurs only in retrospect. I remember the fine times I had on location in Hawaii, the great winters of shooting in the Caribbean, the interesting places all over the United States; the great people that I directed, including Mahalia Jackson, Bess Meyerson, Charlie Ruggles, Vincent Price, Betsy Palmer, Mike Wallace, Betty Furness, and many others. If I think real hard I can also remember the sleepless nights and the constant worry about plans that might go wrong (and sometimes did). Good production is the result of attention to detail. When the shooting starts, everything must be ready. The only thing that cannot be controlled is the weather.

In recent years, production has ended with the delivery of the synced work print and sound track to the agency. From this point on, the process becomes postproduction: the editing of the production elements and the mechanical procedures that are necessary to deliver an approved answer print or videotape master to the advertising agency for broadcasting. Postproduction is an extremely important part of making a television commercial, though it does not have the glamour or financial risk of the actual production. After all, the editor can only work with the material supplied by the director.

CHAPTER

FILM POSTPRODUCTION

Postproduction has become a distinct and specialized part of film making. Television commercials were a major contributing factor to this separation. The advertising agencies started requesting specific editors for their commercials. These editors were not always employees of the company producing the commercial. In addition, the agencies were unhappy with the amount of time their supervisory teams spent away from the office supervising postproduction in distant production centers. It was necessary to produce on location (Los Angeles is the major production center) because of weather, scenery, casting, and technicians; but the time-consuming postproduction, or finishing, could be done close to home with an independent editorial service. This also simplified the approval procedures. Some production companies still do postproduction, but the separate postproduction service is now a major part of the television-commercial industry.

POSTPRODUCTION BIDDING

Most television commercial production is bid up to and including "dailies only," with the commercial to be completed by a finishing or editorial service. Postproduction companies start with an approved work print supplied by the production company and deliver a composite answer print to the advertising agency when the job is completed.

The bidding of postproduction services in film production is not extremely competitive, as all prices are comparable. The intangible of bidding is the editor. At least two bids should be procured to insure that there is an adequate budget for completion of production and delivery of the finished commercial. Most advertising agencies have established a good relationship with a select group of very competent film editors who are backed up by good organizations. It is still an excellent idea to have a price from the editorial service that lists the following

87

elements of production with separate costs for each (all of which will be discussed in this chapter):

Interpositives
Artwork
High-contrast titles
Matte work
High-contrast lab work
Optical negative
Action print only (APO)
Recording and mixing (unless agency supplied)
Mixed magnetic master tracks and copies
Corrected print for tape transfer
Optical sound transfers
Answer prints
Editorial hours
Shipping and delivery

Even when the production company is contracted for postproduction, it is a good idea to separate the finishing charges from the production charges and have an acceptable editor specified in the bid. (The above list applies only to film postproduction; videotape postproduction of film is covered separately in Chapter 7.)

EDITING

I once directed a series of four commercials for International Harvester that were standard truck-demonstration spots. They were rather typical scripts, with running shots, happy driver reactions, closeups of radiators and tires, and a variety of general shots while a voice-over narrator extolled the virtues of the models shown. I photographed the script, screened the dailies, turned everything over to the editor, and thought no more of the project until I was notified that one of the spots had won an award. In disbelief I screened a final print. To my surprise the five-scene spot had been transformed into a quick-cut montage with a full music score, singers, sound effects, and many visual special effects (callled opticals because they are made optically in postproduction). The editor had created a great commercial and I received the credit.

The editor often has considerable influence over a commercial's look, and postproduction is very much his or her domain, whether operating alone or in a salon complete with assistants, negative cutters, and projectionists. In five minutes anyone can learn to splice pieces of film together, but the gift of a good editor is to join them in a way that enhances the spot. Questions such as "Does it flow?," "Does it move?," and "Does it work?" are answered. The commercial editor is actually a second director within the limits of the supplied footage.

Many times a director is also involved in editing, and, at the very least, the director should review all takes with the editor. The Directors Guild contract even specifies that the first editorial version be approved by the director. Advertising agencies do not always concede this authority to the director, and many times a director is not involved in postproduction unless a major problem arises.

Because the agency producer, creative director, writer, and director may all struggle for their cut in an editing room, it helps if the editor is good at personnel relations. An editor must also have a technical knowledge of sound and an ear to wrest a good mix from a sound studio. He or she must have an eye educated to the color balance of scene-to-scene changes—the editor is responsible for the final print's appearance—and a knowledge of graphics in order to choose appropriate type styles and other graphic material for integration into the final spot. Above all, the editor must be a master of scheduling, working on perhaps four or five spots at once using diverse elements that are ordered from the laboratory, art studios, animation services, and sound studios. Finally, the editor must make sure that the finished commercial is delivered by air date.

An editor's equipment has grown from the scissors and cement bottle that were the cutter's tools in early film days to the wide assortment of sophisticated bench consoles in use today. The standard editing machine for the past fifty years was the upright film transport and viewer called the Moviola (Figure 5-1). It was very adequate for the editor working on a motion picture with a director; but in television commercials a number of people are involved in the editing, and it is necessary to have a much larger image for group viewing. Fast rewinding and reviewing of the many reels of work prints is also a requirement, and more than a dozen manufacturers of flatbed editing consoles, including the Moviola Company, compete for this market. Although the old Moviolas are still in use, flat-bed consoles have become standard in commercial postproduction (Figure 5-2).

Film editing is interesting and easily understood. First, all the footage is viewed by the client, the director, and the editor. Comments made during this viewing are almost as important as the script notes. The "I like that" and "Don't use that" statements must be considered, as must the position of the individual making the comments. After the film has been screened, the editor selects the best takes and places them in a readily accessible position. This is

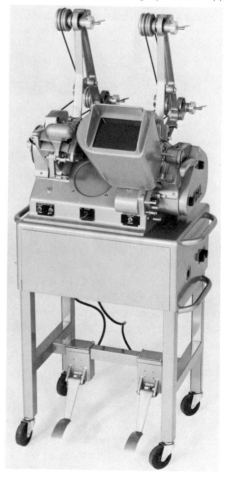

(Courtest Magnasync/Moviola Corp.)

Figure 5-1. The tradiational upright Moviola editing machine with one picture head and one sound head.

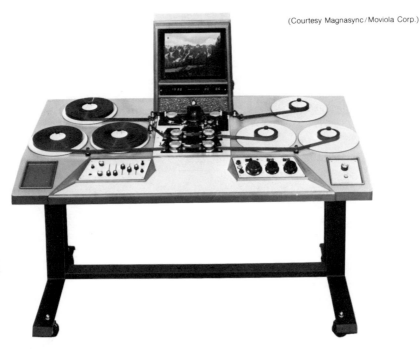

Figure 5-2. Moviola six-plate flat-bed editing console.

usually on pins in a film basket, where they can be visually inspected or spliced in rolls for console use. This hand inspection and random access is one of the joys of film postproduction.

The editor reviews each scene and splices it to the accompanying scenes with perforated Mylar tape. As it is run and rerun, the cut may be easily changed and respliced. The sound must be edited at the same time if sync sound is desired; voice-over sound is not usually edited a great deal. After hours of recutting and viewing, the print is ready to be shown as an edited work print (also called first cut, rough cut, or interlock). At this stage changes can be made without incurring major costs.

The edited work print is usually projected on a large screen. The film projector runs separately from the sound, but the two machines are interlocked so that they run at the same speed, enabling sound to remain in sync with picture. Sometimes this screening takes place on the editor's console rather than in a screening room. This method of review does not have the quality of projection, but it expedites corrections, for the editor can make them on the spot. Final work-print screening should be in a projection room with a good-sized screen so the edited work print can be analyzed in detail.

In the editing of television commercials as in the directing of them, there are no hard-and-fast rules. The creativity of both director and editor is an important factor in producing outstanding commercials, but knowledge of the technical aspect of postproduction is also a necessity. When editing has been completed and the edited work print approved by the client, the printing negative that incorporates all agreed-upon visual effects is prepared. Simple effects are marked on the work print; more complicated instructions are written out in full and either taped to the work print or included on an accompanying instruction sheet (Figures 5-3 and 5-4). No matter how complicated these effects might be, they are all made by rephotographing original material one frame at a time through a critical system of lenses, light sources, and closely calibrated film movements called an optical bench. Because of this procedure, the resulting negative is called an optical negative.

MAKING THE OPTICAL NEGATIVE

Opticals are one of the least-understood ingredients of film making. Many well-established and knowledgeable members of the film industry are not sure how opticals are made. Visual effects created on an optical bench are particularly important in television commercials because of the need for including many images in a short period of time.

Optical negatives not only contain special visual effects, but they also deal with the unexpected and offer solutions to problems that originate in the shoot. One example was a bank commercial shot a few years ago. The production company had completed the photography and the agency had approved it, but a member of the bank's board of directors strongly disapproved of the last scene, in which a tractor moved across a wheat field. It seemed the bank director was connected with a rival tractor firm. A live reshoot was no answer—the season had changed and no wheat fields were available. The answer was an optical that masked out the tractor's nameplate but kept the rest of the scene. This is an example of an expensive repair job done to a relatively modest spot, but opticals can also be economical measures. Imagine a celebrity commercial shot before the product was repackaged. A live reshoot would be very costly, but an optical that changed the package would be relatively inexpensive.

Both these examples use image-replacement mattes that mask out portions of the picture (Figure 5-5). The following is a list of the more common classifications of optical effects and the reasons for using them in commercials:

Transitional effects: The fade, dissolve, wipe, push off, ripple, out of focus, and page turn are only a few of the standard available effects used by most optical houses. Their primary use is to show passage of time and serve as punctuation.

Repositions and blowups: These effects are used to eliminate unwanted areas, correct mistakes, make montages, and reposition backgrounds for titles. They are also used to change image size by optical zooming and frame reduction.

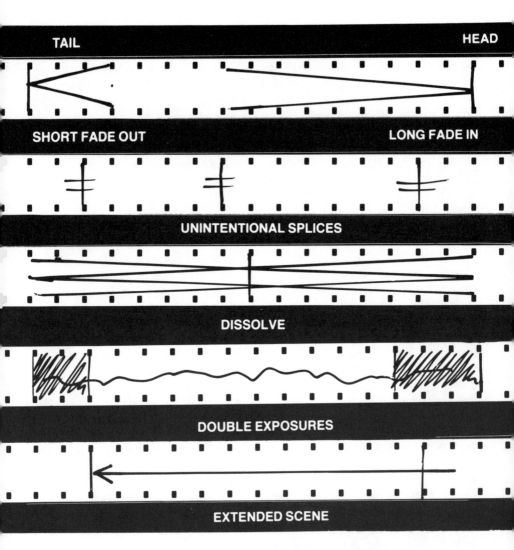

Figure 5-3. Work-print markings for 16-mm and|35-mm standard opticals.

Figure 5-4. A 35-mm work print with special optical instructions indicated.

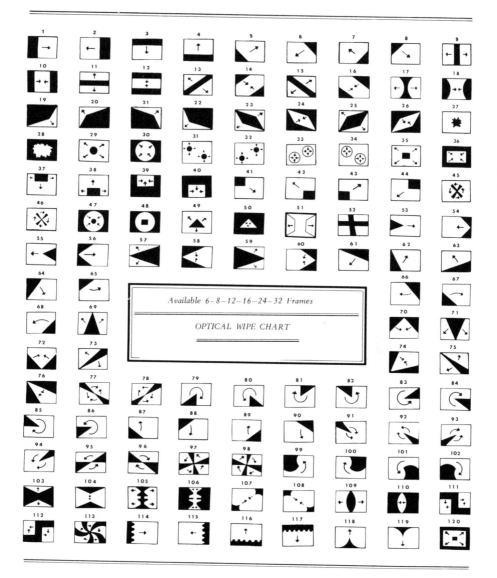

Figure 5-5. Optical wipe chart, typical of most optical companies, showing stock effects from standard mattes on file.

Speed changing: Double-framing or skip-framing slows down or speeds up screen action. Action can also be reversed or frozen.

Double exposure: An image from one or more pieces of film can be overlaid on one piece of film. Snow or rain can be added to a scene, as can a myriad of other similar effects. Many titles are double-exposed.

Changes of quality: This works both ways. Through use of diffusion, filters, dodging, and film-stock choice, beautiful new footage can be made to look like old-time movies, and films with abrasions and scratches can be salvaged on an optical bench that has liquid or immersion film gate apertures on its projectors. This procedure involves an extra charge, but it gives dramatic results on abused negatives.

Image replacement: This type of optical makes a composite picture from a number of sources. Various types of mattes are used to mask out areas of separate pictures and combine them optically into one. This is very critical work and not for the amateur.

All optical work is controlled by the edge numbers incorporated onto the original film during manufacture. These numbers are consecutive at one-foot intervals and print through on the original work print; as the editor selects portions of scenes, rearranges them, and makes a final edit, the edge numbers are the only way that the correct sections of the original negative can be located when the marked-up work print is ready for opticals.

Before an optical can be made, the negative scenes with the same edge numbers as the edited print are sent to the laboratory for a special positive that can be rephotographed with a minimum loss of picture quality. This print is referred to as an interpositive (IP) and is only used for duplication. It is usually made on a special printer called a registration printer to ensure that the pictures are always steady and remain in register with the other pictures. Lettering and title work is usually photographed on black-and-white high-contrast film. Mattes are also photographed on high-contrast film so the black areas are completely opaque and the clear areas are clear.

After the laboratory work is completed, the rolls of film are spliced together in the same order as the work print. IPs are on one roll, black-and-white high-contrast lettering and mattes on a second roll, and a third roll holds double-exposure material such as burn-in titles. The optical layout person analyzes the work print and optical instructions and specifies, on a layout sheet, the procedures for shooting the optical (Figure 5-6). All instructions on this sheet are based on the frame count in the various rolls. All planning is on the layout sheet; the optical-bench operator follows the numbers blindly, going forward, backward, changing exposures, repositioning, putting in filters, reloading, and always checking the numbers on the optical bench. When the optical is completely photographed on the bench, the resulting camera negative should have the correct number of frames exposed so it can be unloaded and sent to the laboratory for development and a check print.

An optical bench is basically a so-

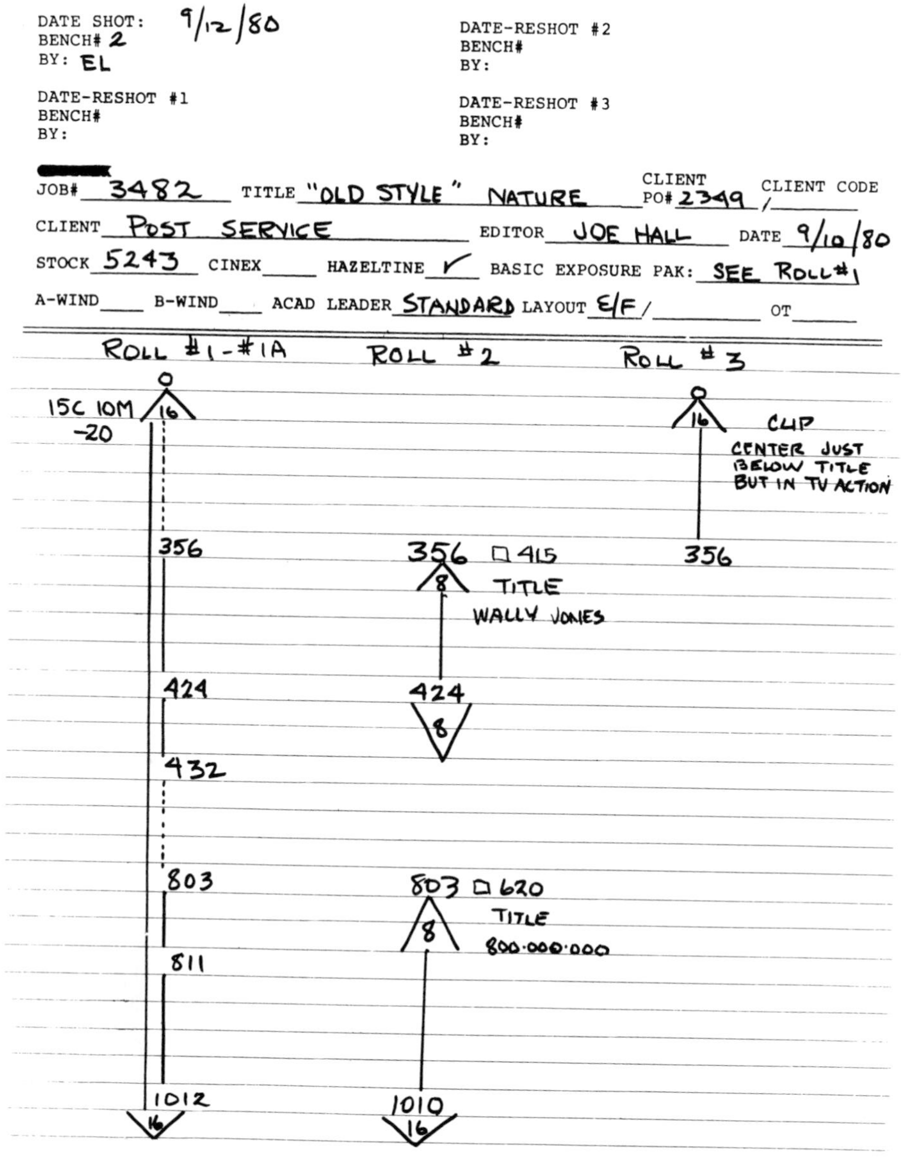

DATE SHOT: 9/12/80
BENCH# 2
BY: EL

DATE-RESHOT #2
BENCH#
BY:

DATE-RESHOT #1
BENCH#
BY:

DATE-RESHOT #3
BENCH#
BY:

JOB# 3482   TITLE "OLD STYLE" NATURE   CLIENT PO# 2349 / _____   CLIENT CODE

CLIENT POST SERVICE   EDITOR JOE HALL   DATE 9/10/80

STOCK 5243   CINEX_____   HAZELTINE ✓   BASIC EXPOSURE PAK: SEE ROLL#1

A-WIND_____   B-WIND_____   ACAD LEADER STANDARD   LAYOUT E/F / _____   OT_____

ROLL #1 - #1A   ROLL #2   ROLL #3

15C 10M /16   /16   CLIP
  -20   CENTER JUST
                           BELOW TITLE
                           BUT IN TV ACTION

356   356 □ 415   356
             /8\   TITLE
                   WALLY JONES

424   424
             \8/

432

803   803 □ 620
             /8\   TITLE
                   800·000·000
811

1012   1010
\16/   \16/

Figure 5-6. A sample optical layout sheet. The frame numbers indicated are from the start marks on all rolls.

phisticated motion-picture copy camera. It has many capabilities and, like animation stands, has become computerized. Because an optical bench deals in 16-mm and 35-mm elements, its adjustments are much more critical than those on an animation stand that photographs 11-by-14-inch cells. Camera and copy movements on an animation stand are in fractions of an inch, but movements on an optical bench are sometimes only a fraction of a millimeter.

The typical optical bench is made up of a main projector with light source, a second projector, and an optical camera (Figure 5-7). Optical elements are threaded on the projectors and photographed one frame at a time according to the instructions on the optical layout sheet. All projectors have separate motors to advance and back up film, move in and out, and lock with each other as the operator wishes. Even on the most automated benches, minute adjustments must be set by hand, and the operator must throw various switches to activate motors. The counters on the projectors must be checked against the

Figure 5-7. A typical optical bench. This bench is a little longer than usual, permitting extreme in-and-out camera movement.

camera counter and the layout sheet at all times. It takes a special type of patience to be an optical person.

Matte work probably evolved from the old movie days, when large sheets of glass plates were rigidly mounted a few feet in front of a motion-picture camera that was set up to photograph a partial set. An artist painted an appropriate picture upon portions of the glass, and the painting obscured and extended portions of the scene. By viewing the scene through the camera, the artist could accurately match and extend the perspective, color, brightness, and overall appearance of the visible set and save thousands of dollars of set construction. Producers of the *Star Wars* films use some glass-plate shots for their backgrounds, but television commercials use the optical matte system to achieve similar results.

Photographing mattes on the optical bench is rather routine; making the mattes themselves is an art. The matte is essentially a silhouette that keeps a portion of the motion-picture frame unexposed so a second exposure can be made in the identical area. There are two ways of making a matte: photographically and by hand.

Making a matte photographically usually entails the use of the cobalt-blue background process. The original photography of the foreground subject is photographed in front of a cobalt-blue background. The subject is lit in a standard manner but the background is lit with a strong blue light. When this negative is printed on high-contrast black-and-white film stock, only the blue background regis-

ters. The developed black-and-white stock has a perfect clear silhouette of the subject; when printed, a perfect black silhouette results. These are the "hold-back" and "see-through" mattes necessary for optical work.

The hand method is called Roto-scoping. The scene to be matted is projected on a drawing surface. Objects to be matted are traced and carefully painted in black on a white drawing surface. If the object is stationary, only one drawing is necessary; if it moves, a drawing is necessary for every frame of the final optical. These drawings are then photographed one frame at a time on high-contrast black-and-white film. The resulting high-contrast negative and a print from it serve as the hold-back and see-through mattes necessary for this type of optical. All projection and photography must be made with registered material on equipment designed for this purpose.

In preparation for shooting the optical, all high-contrast scenes and the IPs are spliced on separate rolls that agree with the optical layout sheets. Once the shooting of the optical begins, frame counters are the only guide to what is happening in the optical camera. The layout sheet is followed exactly. When everything has been completely shot according to the sheet, the film is removed and sent to the lab for developing. If everything is good, this developed negative will be used for printing, and is referred to as the optical negative.

To clarify the matte-making procedure in shooting an optical, here is a simple diagram of the steps necessary for combining a photograph of an airplane with a background picture of clouds (Figure 5-8).

The main projector (roll 1) has the IP of the cloud background and the second projector (roll 1A) has the hold-back matte for the aircraft; they are photographed together on the first pass of the camera. The camera is then rewound to start and the two projectors are reset with the IP of the aircraft in the main projector (roll 2) and the see-through matte in the front projector (roll 2A). When this is photographed, the combined developed negative will contain all the elements. Many optical effects involve this matte process and all involve the creation of an optical negative.

There are times in postproduction when it is necessary to combine animation and live action. Kelloggs' Tony the Tiger and Snap, Crackle, and Pop commercials are examples of character animation combined with live action; the combination of design artwork and live action is very familiar. This combining is generally accomplished by the standard optical procedure, using animation and mattes supplied by the animation studio in conjunction with live action footage. But it can also be achieved by photographing cell artwork (drawings on clear acetate) on an aerial-image animation stand using live footage as a background. The background scene is projected one frame at a time on the

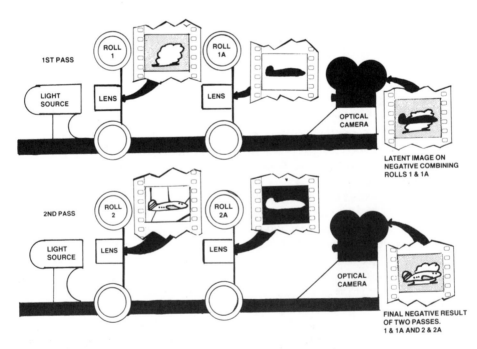

Figure 5-8. Procedures in making a matte shot.

aerial-image stand, on the same plane that the individually drawn cells are placed. Both images are simultaneously photographed one frame at a time. Since the cells are transparent except for areas containing the art, the resulting single-frame photography combines the projected image and the drawings on a single piece of film (Figure 5-9).

The editor must have a thorough understanding of all these optical and laboratory procedures to be truly a director of postproduction. Because instructions change during postproduction, the editor must be aware of any change that might affect the quoted postproduction price.

When the optical negative has been exposed, it is sent to the laboratory for developing and a check print. This first print is made only to check the accuracy of the optical work; because it is only a picture check, it is referred to as an APO (action print only). Under the pressure of schedules, the APO is sometimes combined with a magnetic sound track on videotape and sent to the stations. This is not a good practice, however, for scene-to-scene color and density correction should be made on the optical check print before broadcasting. The term "slop print" is sometimes used for APO; this derogatory phrase undoubtedly keeps many optical check prints from being aired or shown to a client.

After all of the timing corrections have been made, the optical printing negative is ready to be combined with the negative photographic sound (called an optical sound track) to make the final sound-on-film (SOF) re-

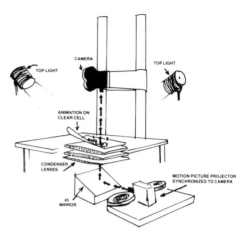

Figure 5-9. Aerial-image animation.

lease prints. Making these sound tracks is also part of postproduction.

SOUND WORK

The sound track is often slighted in TV-commercial production. This is unfortunate, for the sound track should be an effective sales contact without pictures. In the early broadcast days, television commercials were simply visualized radio commercials; many still are.

There are two basic categories of commercial voice tracks—synchronous and voice-over. Synchronous sound is recorded at the same time that the pictures are photographed, and voice-over tracks are usually made in an audio studio. Frequently, advertising agencies produce voice-over tracks and supply the postproduction company with a finished track. Most original sound is recorded on ¼-inch magnetic tape. Small portable recorders like the Nagra are used for sync-sound recording (Figure 5-10); voice-over tracks are usually made with the larger console tape decks (Figure 5-11). Whatever type ¼-inch recorders are used, the recording tape must include a regular pulse signal recorded at the same time as the basic recording. This pulse is originated by the power source and guarantees that picture and sound will be in sync.

Figure 5-10. The very popular Nagra recorder is used for location and studio recordings.

After the sound is recorded on ¼-inch magnetic tape, it is transferred to 35-mm or 16-mm perforated magnetic film for final editing. Because the speed of the ¼-inch recording is controlled by a pulse in transferring, the magnetic film matches the picture frame for frame. It is from these sound tracks that the final mix is made.

The sound track and picture print must always remain in sync during editing. The start of each scene usually has a visual mark on the picture and an audio signal on the track so an exact sync can be established for the scene. The editor places matching marks on both picture and sound every time an edit is made, so even a section trimmed off a scene can be kept in sync. In an emergency, picture and sound can be matched by watching lips and movement and sliding the track to correspond with the same sound.

All equipment used for sound editing, including scissors, splicers, synchronizers, rewinds, and sound reader heads, should be demagnetized at regular intervals. If this is not done, magnetic tracks will pick up unwanted noises.

Figure 5-11. The Studer audio recorder, a studio unit used for announcers, off-camera performers, and sound effects.

Music

Either stock music or original music is used for most television commercials. Stock music is prerecorded music available for television use by paying its owner, a music library, a use fee. The library is responsible for payment of any residuals or composer royalties. These stock orchestrations are on either disk or tape, and the editor dubs them onto magnetic film. Because fees for this type of music are based on the selections used, the cost of music for the spot varies; generally it averages $500 per commercial. Most audio studios carry a full selection of library music.

The editing of library music is a skill that is rather unique. A good music editor can cut on the proper beat and the proper chord so that the music seems to be made for the spot. Many times a number of separate tracks will be used for the music, and during the mix the sound engineer dissolves from one track to another; this is referred to as a segue by sound mixers.

Original music scores are generally made after the commercial has been completely edited. The composer notes all the action and takes a frame count. Each bit of action is associated with the proper frames. Because the number of frames determines screen time, the composition of the music track can match the picture to the frame. A piano track will usually be submitted for approval. This track will be on magnetic film so that it can be interlocked with the completed workprint cut. If approved, the music will be arranged for the different musicians and a recording session set.

The composer relates frame count to commercial time. Since film is projected at twenty-four frames per second, a twelve-frame beat is half a second, an eight-frame beat is one-third of a second, and so forth. During the recording session, the conductor and the instrumentalists hear the same specified beat (or rhythm) through one earphone. If the correct mechanical beat is fed to the musicians, and the music has been composed properly, the music will match the picture exactly.

In the recording session, the conductor alerts all the musicians, gives the countdown, and the music is played and recorded (Figures 5-12 and 5-13). If a playback is approved, musicians are dismissed and the tape is turned over to the finishing company for mixing. If budget permits, running the work print during the recording is helpful. Seeing the picture and music together at this point seems to help the conductor make better music.

Original-music recording is a very enjoyable part of commercial production; everyone involved in this phase is a true professional. The American Federation of Musicians has many rules regarding performance and residuals. The music company or composer is obliged to conform to these rules; they are signatories to the contract. The agency is responsible for the payment of residuals when the commercial is used.

Jingles and music used for studio playing back during photography are grouped together because both are original and prerecorded. In one respect, jingles are a radio-type track: remembering the audio message is all-important, and the pictures are usually visualizations of the familiar musical theme. The sound track becomes the guide for editing, and the pictures are cut to it. A voice-over announcer can be added to the jingle during the final mix.

Figure 5-12. A twenty-four channel mixing console used in music recording.

Figure 5-13. A twenty-four-channel audio tape recorder used in music recording.

Playing back prerecorded music during photography allows the on-camera players to keep time to the music or even mouth the words as if they were singing. This is a standard method of production in film musicals. The complete track is played for each take, and the countdown on the sound track is matched to a visual count-down so the editor can keep everything in proper synchronization. The played-back track is not recorded; the original track is used for editing.

Sound Mixing

In recent years there have been many advances in sound recording.

Digital recording and multiple-channel recording are but two. No matter what technical equipment is used, sound elements must be balanced, compressed, sweetened, and mixed together to arrive at the final sound on a single magnetic or optical track that will be broadcast. This procedure is called mixing and it is controlled by the studio sound mixer or mixing engineer.

In the final mix of sound, the mixing engineer, the editor, and all concerned agency personnel view the picture while all the sound tracks are played on separate channels and blended together. The typical mixing studio has a large screen for viewing the picture with interlocked sound, a footage counter beneath the screen, a good speaker system, and an audio-mixing console of at least twelve channels (Figure 5-14). The mixing engineer must be mechanically competent in electronics and must also have experience and judgment to know the best balance of tracks for television commercials (Figure 5-15). Knowledge of the quality of sound on the home television set is an extremely important asset too, and many sound studios play the final mix through a small speaker that duplicates this quality. An ability to handle people is also a plus.

The mixing log prepared by the editor includes all footage, contents of individual tracks, and fade and cross-dissolve suggestions accurately designated (Figure 5-16). The mixer (or mixing engineer) can reduce recording time significantly with a professional log. An accurate mixing log not

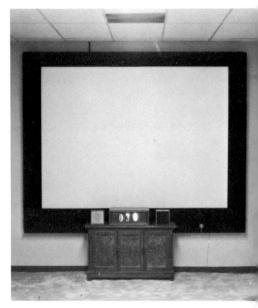

Figure 5-14. Projection screen at Universal Recording used to view picture while mixing sound tracks. Below the screen is a footage counter and two three-inch speakers for sound playback.

Figure 5-15. A sixteen-channel mixing console used for multiple-magnetic-track mixing to picture. Notice the spectrum analyzer in the background; this gives a visual frequency response.

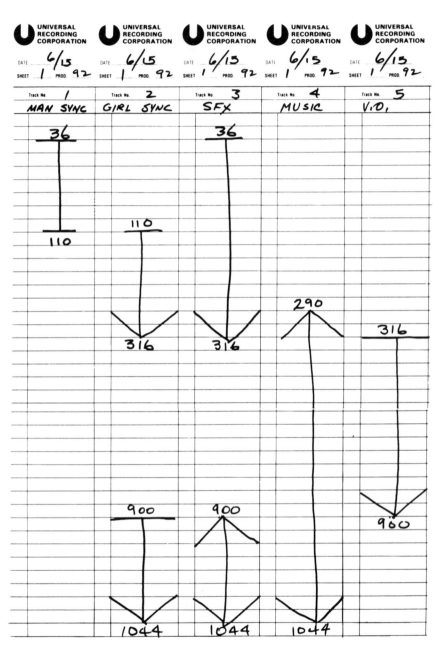

Figure 5-16. A simple rerecording mixing log. The numbers on the log are 35-mm footages measured from the start mark of each reel.

only eliminates a lot of unnecessary conversation between mixer and supervisors, it also shows the particular sound on each channel and saves a lot of search time.

A very simple mix can be completed within one hour with one mixer. It takes considerably more time when a large number of tracks are used or when mixing each track involves special corrections. In some cases, a premix or more than one mixer may be necessary (Figure 5-17).

The first run-through usually produces a dissonant combination of sounds as the mixer finds the levels for all the tracks and checks the mixing log. The second run is occasionally a "keeper," but it usually takes at least three attempts before a good mix is achieved. This mix must pass the critical ears of the agency supervisors as it is replayed with the picture. Time in a mixing studio is charged by the hour, and one thirty-second spot usually takes one hour. After a mix has an official OK, it is ready for transferring to optical film, or for being used as is in a videotape product.

Figure 5-17. The master control room at Universal Recording. In the center is the patching panel for all equipment; on the left wall are some of the playback machines.

An optical sound transfer is a transfer of the sound signal on the magnetic tape to a sound signal on photographic film. The sound on the magnetic film controls the action of an exposure light in a 16-mm or 35-mm sound recording camera. The exposed film is developed to a high contrast (Figure 5-18). Prints from this negative are run on a projector where the sound track passes between a constant intensity lamp and a photoelectric cell. The variations of light intensity on the photo cell are amplified to reproduce the original sound. Combining this optical negative with the picture negative in printing results in a composite (picture and sound) print (Figure 5-19).

Although the finishing company has specifications for the optical sound transfer, it is a good idea to understand television station requirements for 16-mm prints and how they are met.

Television stations require B-wind prints for broadcast. This means that they need a 16-mm print that is projected with the emulsion facing the lens. To end up in this position, a contact print must be printed from an A-wind negative picture and track. Original camera negative in 16-mm is B wind, so an intermediate step must be taken to arrive at the correct wind for television prints; 16-mm reduction prints are generally B wind (Figure 5-20).

Television stations demand B-wind prints because their projectors cannot be refocused between every spot, and they want the emulsion facing the same way on all film commercials. A-

wind and B-wind prints can be distinguished in the following way: when the film is projected and the emulsion faces the lens and screen it is a B-wind print but if the support (shiny) side faces the lens and screen it is an A-wind print. Although most station distribution is now on videotape, many smaller stations still use film.

Figure 5-18. 16-mm and 35-mm optical sound tracks on film negatives.

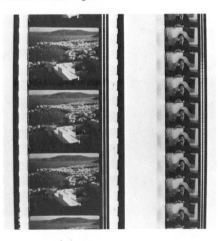

Figure 5-19. Composite film prints in 16-mm and 35-mm; these are also referred to as SOF (sound-on-film) prints.

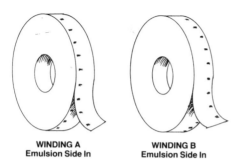

WINDING A
Emulsion Side In

WINDING B
Emulsion Side In

Figure 5-20. The traditional illustration of A-wind and B-wind. Television stations require B-wind prints.

LABORATORY PROCEDURES

The motion-picture laboratory is where all the pieces are put together. The chemistry of photography is extremely critical, but the motion-picture laboratory is a consistently stable part of television-commercial production. The freedom and creative aspects of photography, editing, and sound can only be fulfilled in association with a good laboratory. The basic laboratory operations are:

1. Developing original camera negative
2. Work-printing the original negative
3. Making master intermediate positive (IP) for optical effects
4. Developing the optical negative made by the optical company
5. Printing a check print (APO or "slop print") from the optical negative
6. Making a composite (picture and sound) answer print from the optical negative and the photographic sound track
7. On approval of answer print, making the printing materials necessary for quantity printing
8. Making quantity prints

Each step in the laboratory procedure takes an established amount of time to complete. Because scheduling is extremely important in commercial production, an understanding by editor and agency producer of what occurs in the allotted time is a necessity.

Developing Original Camera Negatives

The importance of this first step is self-evident (Figure 5-21). Unless otherwise specified, all negative film is developed in standard fashion, but there are many options available (Figure 5-22). For example, it can be developed to double the negative's rated speed; this is called "pushing one stop." It can also be developed to halve the speed of the basic film; this is referred to as low-contrast developing. Original negative film has been ruined in a laboratory, but with a good lab this is a rare occurrence.

Figure 5-21. Darkroom loading area in a motion-picture laboratory. The room is normally in total darkness with the raw-stock supply reels on the left, the storage elevators in the center, and the first developer tank on the right.

Figure 5-22. The lightroom at a motion-picture laboratory. In the background is a film-drying cabinet; in the foreground, the processing tanks that precede the drying.

Work-printing the Original Negative

A daily or work print is made from the camera negative immediately after the negative has been developed. Before proper printing instructions can be determined, the negative must be viewed on a machine that converts the negative to positive (reverses polarity) and has variable settings that correspond to the laboratory printers. This piece of equipment is called an analyzer and is basically a closed-circuit television system. The most popular of these analyzers is made by the Hazeltine Company and called a Hazeltine.

Properly operated, analyzers are extremely accurate in balancing or timing negatives for density and color (Figure 5-23).

Making the Master Intermediate Positive (IP)

The negative is timed on the Hazeltine analyzer and then printed on a registration printer using low-contrast duplicating film stock and developed in negative chemistry (Figure 5-24). The result is a positive material that can be used to make negatives with a minimal loss of quality.

Figure 5-23. Timing a negative on a Hazeltine color analyzer. The negative is placed over an aperture in the foreground and the reversed picture appears on the monitor. The picture on the left is projected for reference.

Figure 5-24. A 35-mm registration printer used in the making of registered intermediate positives (IPs).

Developing the Optical Negative

This negative is developed under the stringent controls used with all negatives.

Printing the APO

This is the optical negative check print. It is usually a rough one-light print that is timed on the analyzer for overall density and color. It is a quick print made from the optical negative.

Making a Composite Answer Print

The optical negative is timed scene-by-scene and combined with a sound track optical negative to make an answer print for client approval. This answer print can be a 35-mm contact composite, a 16-mm contact composite, or a 16-mm reduction composite. A contact print is printed in contact with the original printing material; a reduction print is reduced from a 35-mm original to a 16-mm print for viewing convenience.

Making Printing Materials

Because the optical negative is very valuable, quantity printing should be made from a duplicate; continuous use of a negative in printing creates abrasions. This is particularly true during the printing of reduction prints. This duplicate material can be made either through a positive to negative process or through a color reversal intermediate (CRI) process. The CRI film eliminates the positive step in negative duplication; the commercial goes from negative to negative. The CRI is mainly used for duplicate printing negatives.

Making Quantity Prints

Quantity prints can be made in a few days from the approved material. When the requested prints have been delivered, printing elements should be returned from the laboratory to the postproduction company. Most production companies hold this material as long as they are working with the account. Six months has been established as the minimum time a postproduction company must store printing elements. It is the advertising agency's responsibility to inform the production company regarding the disposition of printing material after this time has elapsed. Storage companies will store this material in film vaults for a small monthly charge per can. The storage and distribution of both film and videotape material is covered in detail in Chapter 7.

The use of videotape in postproduction of filmed commercials has become popular in recent years. This type of film finishing, referred to as electronic editing, is explained in Chapter 7.

CHAPTER

VIDEOTAPE PRODUCTION

For more than half a century, film was the only medium for recording moving pictures with sound. With the arrival of television broadcasting, a new recording technique was needed. Since all television sound and pictures were basically electrical impulses, it did not take long for electrical engineers to adapt the established audio tape-recording material to the electrical signals of television and successfully record both pictures and sound. Video is the word used to describe the visual portion of a TV broadcast, and the material that can record both picture and sound is called videotape.

Many companies that specialize in production of television commercials call themselves film and videotape production companies. Actually, most of these suppliers do not own videotape equipment because of the tremendous cost; rather, they rent hardware and technical personnel from a videotape facility in the same manner as they rent cameras for film production. Television commercials produced on videotape are usually shot with cinematic (one-camera) technique; the separate scenes are edited after production. The price for videotape production charged by a commercial production company is approximately the same as film for a comparable spot, because the money saved on film laboratory work is counterbalanced by the rental of video equipment and technicians. The film and videotape production company marks up all costs as part of its price.

One type of videotape production allows a considerable price savings—working directly with a full-service videotape company and bypassing the television-commercial production company. The videotape industry expanded tremendously in the late 1970s, even though millions of dollars are necessary to set up any type of videotape service and equipment seems to become obsolete as fast as it is installed. Because of the amount of investment necessary for videotape operations, five types of videotape companies are operating: full service, equipment and facility rental, electronic editing, videotape transfer, and dubbing and distribution.

Full-service companies have some staff and complete facilities for any type of videotape production. This usually includes some type of editing. The bulk of a full-service company's income is derived from producing multiple-camera events: football, basketball, and baseball games, musicals, political events, or any other such event is a natural for a local full-service videotape company. The company engaged in this type of taping is left with available time for commercial production.

Cost of production with a full-service operation is determined by number of technicians, equipment, and time. It is very likely that special talent will need to be hired for production of high-quality television commercials. A commercial director is the most important addition to the production crew. There are many free-lance directors available in most production centers; the tape company can recommend some and also has other specialists available on a free-lance basis. For local or low-budget spots, advertising agencies are more and more often using their own staff for producing and directing. With immediate playback of videotape, a great deal of anxiety and mystery has been removed, but it is still necessary to have one person in charge—in essence the director.

This chapter examines television-commercial production with a full-service videotape company. A producer working directly with a full-service videotape company can save money and exert a great deal of personal control over a television commercial. One of the reasons why the cost is relatively lower is the price of labor: most videotape companies have nonunion

staffs because union jurisdictions have not yet been established in the videotape industry. However, the producer must be extremely careful about union conflicts; if film-union personnel are mingled with electronic technicians, the potential problems should be investigated before the shooting day. When an IATSE member is requested by the director as a director of photography, art director, floor mixer, or gaffer, the union must be checked for clearance. The film unions are very interested in employment for their members in this new medium, so mixed crews (union and nonunion) have become very common. In fact, the only major difference between film and videotape commercial production is the camera and method of recording the images.

PREPLANNING

The script and storyboards of a videotape production are identical to the script and storyboards for a film production. The schedule is usually shorter for videotape, and a very careful time watch must be kept. If price is a consideration, bidding must be carefully monitored and all parties must have a complete understanding of their responsibilities. A commercial-production company consistently delivers a higher quality product than a full-service videotape company, but its price is consistently higher. Preplanning meetings with all account, creative, and business groups should be recorded and accompany the bid requests.

Bidding

One bid should be procured from a film and videotape production company that is a reliable supplier; this establishes what production will cost (in the long run this may be the best way). Next, the agency should send the script and storyboard to full-service videotape companies that work directly on the job. A request should be made for a price of production and for a list of the elements that the service will supply and those they expect the agency to supply. Their contribution usually includes equipment and technicians.

The next step is to check available directors. This inquiry can sometimes be done through the tape service or through local listings of free-lance directors. A fee is agreed upon for the director's preshoot days of planning, shoot days, and postshoot days (for supervising editing). It is possible to find a free-lance nonunion director, and a major saving can be realized. The important step is to find a capable director who can devote full time to the project for the contracted period. The director should be experienced in TV commercial directing; a studio videotape director is not usually qualified to direct commercials. Samples of his or her work on film or videotape cassette should be reviewed.

The tape company can supply a lighting technician as part of its proposal, but the director usually prefers to have a director of photography of his or her choosing supervise the lighting. The director of photography may not wish to operate the camera. Since immediate playback is available,

the camera operator's work is quickly reviewed. This operator's cost must be included in the estimate.

Talent agents or casting agencies must be contacted for casting. The auditions can take place at the agency, casting service, or any other convenient place, including motel or hotel rooms.

Sketches of the sets should be checked with the director and client before the tape company starts building; studio and talent should be booked for the necessary shooting days. Props and wardrobe are a necessity for most large-scale productions. Some areas will have free-lance stylists, home economists, and production assistants to work on a per-diem basis.

If the agency works with a DGA signatory, an assistant director or a unit production manager can be hired through the Guild to pull the job together. The tape company should have its own production person assigned to coordinate all the elements within the tape service. Costs of special lighting equipment and cameras, lenses, and accessories must be considered and estimated.

The on-camera talent, if they are professionals, will be AFTRA members and must be paid by a signatory to the AFTRA agreements. Ordinarily the agency is a signatory; if not, talent and residual companies can perform this service for a small fee.

The tape company estimates its editing time based on experience and gives a price. All aspects of production must be cost-estimated. The standard production-company markup is not applied to videotape production, but the saving may be less than one expects: my experience has shown that after the agency figures the total cost and schedule, it would do well to add 10 percent to the cost and two days to the overall schedule.

EQUIPMENT

Videotape language is very different from film language; this is especially true of equipment. Equipment is the backbone of the electronics industry and is a source of conflict between technicians and the creative group. One way to bridge this gap is for everyone to learn some of the tape language.

The videotape recorder is referred to as the VTR, and the combination of portable camera and ¾-inch recorder is referred to as electronic news gathering, or ENG. The small camera can also be used with 2-inch recorders (called quad because they record with four high-speed rotating heads) or 1-inch recorders, in which case it is electronic field production or EFP. The reliable quad is the workhorse of the broadcast industry. Its drawbacks are its extreme cost, lack of portability, and operating cost. VTRs in ¾-inch or ½-inch are very popular with the general public, but are far from broadcast quality. The latest breakthrough in VTR is the 1-inch helical scan. Properly maintained and used, it is every bit as good as a 2-inch and, in many cases, far superior (Figure 6-1). The best high-quality services usually have 1-inch VTRs for location work and either 1-inch or 2-inch VTRs for studio work. The time projection for replace-

ment of all 2-inch with 1-inch equipment is 1985.

The television camera is the first part of the videotape system and must be of the highest quality. There are many excellent cameras, and the tape service has cameras matched to its VTRs (Figure 6-2). The camera usually has a small black-and-white viewer for the operator, but a large color set should be available for playback of all recorded takes and constant monitoring of new ones. In some situations, NG takes are erased, but the history of TV production has shown that many times the mistakes are the scenes used. Therefore, it is more common to save all takes for future review. Two-inch tape costs about $300 a reel, and one-inch tape is about half that price; operational economy is another reason for using the smaller format.

Figure 6-1. This one-inch C-format videotape recorder (VTR) can be used on location or in the studio.

Figure 6-2. The RCA TK-760 video camera is used for studio and location videotaping.

With miniaturized solid-state circuits, it takes the television camera no longer to set up and zero in than it takes a film camera. Because EFP no longer requires large equipment trucks or control rooms, it has become a very practical method of producing television commercials. Electronic technicians maintain picture quality by analyzing the video signals on a scope called a waveform monitor while production is in progress; much time is spent maintaining ·a perfect signal. Many times this signal must be compromised for a picture effect. The scope's little green lines once triggered heated discussions between the director and the chief video engineer.

The video technicians worried more about the signals on the wave-form monitor than the actual picture and the director didn't give a damn about the little green lines.

Some film camermen are resistant to videotape production and the changes it entails. But more and more film cameramen are working with tape, and tape spots exhibit some of the same lighting effects and have an overall look approaching that of film. A film cameraman usually lights a scene to an intensity of about 100 footcandles, the light necessary for standard film emulsions. It is not unusual for a video technician to request more light, usually asking for about 200 footcandles.

On a recent project, the film cameraman, recognizing this pattern, lit the scene to 200 footcandles the first time. In a few moments the video tech appeared on the set, as usual, with a demand for more light.

The communication problem is becoming less major as film people and tape techs become more involved with one another. There seems to be a generation gap between the two groups that only time will cure.

PREPRODUCTION

Videotape preproduction is almost identical to film preproduction, and the same careful planning must be taken. Most television-commercial production companies have a staff that knows preproduction details but working with a full-service videotape production company that is not primarily a commercial producer requires an accurate checklist of the many production details. Let us review the steps that must be taken in a film or videotape production.

Set the dates for shooting. This firmly establishes the complete schedule.

Confirm the director's schedule. Make sure preproduction and postproduction days are specified.

Reserve equipment and studio for the shooting days. This is particularly important with a full-service videotape studio because of the utilization of its equipment. Portable equipment with the proper technicians must also be scheduled for location work.

Search for any needed locations. The videotape studio does not usually accept this responsibility. Location-search companies are available in many sections of the country, and it is the producer's responsibility to find the locations and clear them for shooting.

Hold the production meeting. A complete scene-by-scene review of the commercial should be made with the producer, director, and videotape-service coordinator present. Any special equipment should be requested; videotape equipment such as special cameras, lenses, generators, or recorders are the videotape service's responsibility, and responsibility for other equipment should be established. The shooting schedule should be confirmed.

Cast talent. Ideally, the director should be present at the casting session, and the session should be recorded on a small-format videotape. Wardrobe should be specified and the responsibility for procuring it assigned. The selected performers must be given the call time, conflicts checked, and final scripts handed out for memorizing.

Schedule free-lancers. Anyone not part of the basic videotape crew who is needed must be hired, such as extra production assistants, art director, script clerk, property master, stylist (this could be the art director), makeup artist and hairdresser, floor sound mixer (if videotape sound engineer is not acceptable), home economist (if food preparation is needed).

Double check everything before shooting. Sets should be constructed and propped, locations cleared and dressed. Any location should be checked with the director before being cleared. A release from the owner (there is usually a fee) or written permission from the supervisor of public property (there is usually a permit with fee) is necessary. It is always wise to notify the police (sometimes this means a fee); weather contingencies must always be remembered.

Transportation and meals are part of production. A bus may be the solution to transportation, as parking always seems to be a problem. Catering lunch will speed up production; it can be anything from a "jungle lunch" (fruit, sandwich, milk, cake) to a complete hot table set up by a caterer.

All these steps are identical in film and videotape production. The only difference in the mechanics are the camera and recording material.

Because a great deal of videotape production involves on-camera speakers, an excellent teleprompter system has evolved using a closed-circuit

Figure 6-3. A video prompter. The monitor shows the closed-circuit script; it is reflected on the mirror through which the camera shoots.

black-and-white television camera and monitor (Figure 6-3). The copy is reflected on a partially silvered mirror through which the video camera shoots. The two-way mirror cuts the light a little but the speaker is looking directly into the lens during the speech. This is an advanced adaptation of the mechanical teleprompter used in film production.

If everything is properly organized, the actual shooting of a commercial is somewhat of an anticlimax.

THE VIDEO CAMERA AND VTR

The film camera and the video camera are the same in many ways. The lenses and their mounts are similar; each uses the same filter for the same purpose and each focuses the optical image on a focal plane in the camera. But the focal plane in the film camera is where the unexposed raw stock receives its optical information; the latent image is chemically enhanced until it reproduces on film a negative likeness of the subject in front of the lens. In the video camera, this information is focused on a television tube or tubes that instantly transform it into an electrical signal that can be recorded on magnetic tape. When this tape is played back and the signal amplified, it re-creates the original image on a television monitor. Another difference is that the film camera is both a camera and a film recorder, while the video camera must be connected to a separate magnetic recorder. The magnetic recording of the video image is a two-step operation.

The quality of the video picture is governed by the type of equipment used and the ability of the technicians who operate and maintain it. There are many manufacturers of the three types of video cameras in general use today: the large studio camera, that uses a 1¼-inch pickup tube; the general-purpose camera, with a 1-inch pickup tube; and the portable EFP camera, with a ¾-inch tube (Figure 6-4). The measurements refer to the width of the tube's receiving face and correspond in size to the width of film in a film camera. Film-oriented individuals might think that the larger the pickup tube, the better the picture, but this is not necessarily true. The EFP camera and state-of-the-art general-use cameras all use the smaller tube, and the competition for sales has forced all manufacturers to put most of their design effort into perfecting the smaller format. The EFP camera's small size and excellent pickup tubes are the reasons that most television commercial production uses it.

Although the conversion of the optical signal into an electronic signal occurs in the pickup tube, much sophisticated electronics is necessary to form the composite image on the videotape. The final recording's accuracy depends on the advanced engineering and precision manufacturing of this equipment, but the quality is limited by the 525 horizontal lines that make up the television picture. The recording quality of a good EFP system is probably exceeds the ability of the home TV set to reproduce it.

The demand for motion-picture technicians is decreasing as the need for experienced electronic technicians is increasing. More motion-picture

cameramen are now lighting for and operating videotape cameras than ever before. Years of experience in motion pictures are being applied throughout the complete videotape production spectrum from director to editor; this is one reason for the enormous improvement in production quality. Designers and manufacturers of video cameras are trying to meet the requirements of the motion-picture camera users. Both Panavision and Ikagami are marketing electronic cinematography cameras that, because of lenses, circuitry, and film-style controls, permit filmlike operation and results.

There is no doubt that the new generation of video camera is a great improvement over older ones. Video technicians now relate the sensitivity of their camera pickup tubes to the speed of motion-picture film. This means that the amount of light on a

Figure 6-4. The RCA TK60c portable ENG/EFP video camera.

set necessary for maximum quality from the video camera can be measured with a standard exposure meter. It is then a simple matter to view the picture on the video monitor to check lighting and overall quality.

Video engineers are trained to check their wave-form monitors for accurate readings of each color's individual response (Figure 6-5). These scope readings are the equivalent of the curves on a motion-picture laboratory graph, where each color is analyzed after development. Both methods of color analysis are helpful, but the important picture is the one on the monitor or screen. It is sometimes necessary to compromise the graph lines to get the desired picture.

In the same manner that film can be ''pushed'' to a faster speed, the video camera can boost its picture. Most ENG or EFP cameras have a small switch that can boost sensitivity. As in film, each push deteriorates the quality: in film it causes more ''grain,'' in videotape it causes ''noise.'' One of the benefits of videotape is the ability to view the end result of the push and make a judgment of its acceptability before the scene is recorded.

Modern VTRs match the ability of the video cameras. The traditional two-inch (quad) recorders are still used in the broadcast industry, and much of the studio commercial production goes directly on them. But the one-inch broadcast high-band helical scan recorders are fast making them obsolete. One of the current problems with one-inch recorders is a lack of standardization in the industry. There are two one-inch formats in general

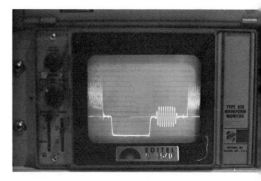

Figure 6-5. A wave-form monitor showing the ''little green lines'' that measure and analyze different parts of the video signal.

use: type B and type C. The type B format was developed by Philips and Bosch-Fernseh and is sometimes referred to as the European system; the type C format is produced by RCA, Sony, and Ampex and has been approved by the Society of Motion Picture and Television Engineers (SMPTE) for general use. Studio and portable units are available in both formats, which unfortunately are not compatible; if original material is recorded on one format, the editing service must have the same type of machine.

SPECIAL VIDEOTAPE TECHNIQUES

There are some unusual production methods that are not used in the typical videotape commercial. Since the EFP cameras are about the same size as film cameras and take the same type of lenses and filters, they can do almost anything that a film camera can do—as long as they are hooked up to a recorder. Thus the special-viewpoint photography that can be achieved with a film camera can usually be made with a video camera.

Image-replacement or traveling mattes are a specialty of the videotape production field. The matte process is referred to as Chroma Key, Image Matte, or Ultimatte. A similar effect would take weeks to complete on film, but it can be realized on videotape with the push of a button. In film, such a composite picture is a post-production operation; on videotape it must be part of the shooting.

Two simultaneous sources of pictures are necessary when shooting mattes on videotape. One camera focuses on the foreground object in front of a well-lit shadowless green or blue background. The second camera focuses on the background scene. Through a special switcher, the image from the first camera is overlaid on the second camera image. The objects in the foreground completely block the background behind them; the picture with its new background can then be viewed on a monitor and recorded if satisfactory. Miniature people with giant products is a common example of this technology; it is also a standard practice on news shows that combine newscasters and events. With proper planning, shadows of the photographed material can follow the contours of the background scene. Planning is always the secret of good production, but it is essential when using these video tricks.

SHOOTING DAY—STUDIO

Before the videotape shooting day begins, everyone involved in the project must understand how the commercial will be produced. A full-service videotape studio facility is accustomed to managing all production from a control booth, with the camera operators and floor manager taking instructions from the director through earphones. The lighting director and performers get their instructions over a loudspeaker. Television-station commercial services have the same system. This is adequate for simple presenter commercials and is necessary for multiple-camera commercials, but a director who specializes in television-commercial production probably prefers to work film style: one camera, a good floor monitor, and direct communication with the performers and technicians.

The first videotape shooting day has the same pressures as film production. Is the director getting things organized? If not, why not? Are the talent, makeup artists, and hairdressers at the studio at call time? Out on the floor, the video technician should be getting the camera ready; this is the first major difference between a film shoot and a videotape shoot (Figure 6-6). A video camera is focused on an illuminated line grid and gray scale, and the technician might drop one side of the camera to make some minor adjustments. On newer camera equipment, a camera control unit (CCU) controls the video camera; this is adjusted until the monitor and the scope meet with the technician's approval. Finally, within an hour, the official word is relayed to the director that "Camera is ready," and an electronic engineer might say, "You have fax," meaning that facilities are available.

The audio engineer checks with the director on how to handle the microphones in a commercial with sync sound. A good mixer usually prefers an open mike on a boom for optimum quality, but if the action or number of microphones makes this impossible, he or she usually settles for hidden button microphones. Sound is such an important part of a TV commercial that it is a wise move to check into a sound person's credentials before the shooting day. A VTR records the sound along with the picture; this means that on a sound-check playback the picture is visible and might create a distraction. I prefer sound playback through earphones without looking at the monitor.

The audio mixer works where the director can communicate with him or her. If budget allows, a protection track should be made on a ¼-inch synchronous-signal tape recorder in addition to the sound feed into the videotape recorder. This has many benefits. Sound can be played back or recorded on set without involving the VTR, and, if the mix is very complicated, it can be transferred to magnetic film and handled like a film mix on magnetic channels without dubbing down from (making a duplicate of) the master videotape.

Because the commercial uses cinematic technique, the familiar clapstick helps sound identification and permits the sound to be separated from the picture without losing sync. A time code should also be put on the videotape while shooting for the same reason. A well-kept script is a big help in the editing of the finished commer-

Figure 6-6. Getting ready to videotape a scene; make-up is preparing talent. Notice the flags used to block light from the Hitachi EFP camera and the shotgun microphone on the boom arm.

cial, because of the detailed logging of each individual scene and the time saved in selecting the good takes.

The lighting director or director of photography supervises the rough lighting of the set and the running of the power lines. Film lighting and videotape lighting are not exactly the same: film can record an extreme range of light intensity, while videotape has a bit of a problem with extreme highlights and very deep shadows. The familiar streaking or comet tailing of overexposed highlights on videotape (caused by a tube burnout) can sometimes be controlled by careful lighting. Some cameras are designed to alleviate this problem and also to hold more shadow detail (this rendition of contrast is one of the ingredients in the film look). Videotape also needs considerably more light than does color film. Fortunately, a good monitor on the set can clarify most problems (Figure 6-7).

Figure 6-7. Videotape support equipment being used on location; it supplements the one-inch recorder.

When the talent is ready for rehearsal, all the equipment should be in working order and zeroed in. As the action develops, most eyes will be on the monitor, not on the actual scene, as in film shooting. There is no mystery now; everyone on the stage can see the lighting, color, action, and camera moves, can hear the sound, and can approve or disapprove.

The director says "Let's go!" The assistant director or a technician orders the set closed and calls for quiet. In the studio the recorder might be far away from the set in an equipment room; therefore, a technician should be on earphones to the video engineer, who is monitoring quality and controlling the recorders. If a video teleprompter is used, the prompter operator should also be on earphones. The director then tells the video engineer to roll the VTR, waits a moment, then calls "Action" and proceeds as if on film until "Cut." Unless all the

equipment is on the shooting stage and everyone can communicate easily, there are always a number of earphones on a videotape studio shoot.

SHOOTING DAY—LOCATION

Working on location is the same for videotape as for film production until the setting up of the camera. As with film, the crew, performers, and equipment must travel to the location and get organized. The location call should be earlier than usual. The videotape camera must be lined up by hand—on the camera itself or remotely with CCUs. Since there are many separate components in a videotape system, it is sometimes wise to use a small van as an equipment room and communicate through earphones and microphones. With one-inch VTRs, it is sometimes practical to set up the equipment in the location (Figure 6-8). Although all equipment, in addition to the recorder, must be removed from the van, the direct communication between the crew and director is a definite plus.

Sync-sound recording on location is sometimes a problem because of extraneous noise. An open mike on a fishpole (hand-held boom) is first choice for sound pickup, but small button microphones that can be placed on the performers must often be used to minimize outside noise. Small radio-microphone transmitters are also frequently used on location to eliminate microphone lines. It is important to have a floor mixer who is concerned with nothing but sound.

Lighting on location is always harder to control than in the studio, and videotape lighting is more critical than film lighting because of problems of contrast and sensitivity. In all location lighting the available power supply must be considered, even though location lights are smaller and take less electricity than studio lights. The video camera can run on batteries (power pack) or use standard sixty-cycle power. Exterior shooting usually requires supplemental lighting to fill in shadows on sunny days or to create a light source on cloudy days. Reflectors are still frequently used to fill in shadows, but an efficient daylight-type lamp called an HMI can be used not only for fill but also as a source. It is not necessary to use a conversion filter on the camera for daylight color (as in film) because color adjustments can be made electronically. The green lines of the wave-form generator scope are a big help in setting the right color for exteriors; everyone's eyes quickly adapt to the cool outside color temperature, and it is difficult to judge color on the picture monitor.

As in any type of shooting, the shot list is followed one scene at a time until the production is completed. With the exception of the special technical equipment, videotape production is the same as film production; the end result is to produce a good advertising message with exceptional competence. Postproduction on videotape, however, is completely different from film postproduction. It is worth noting that production and postproduction of film has been developing since the 1920s while electronic videotape editing is a baby of the late 1970s.

Figure 6-8. An Ikagami EFP camera being used on a location commercial.

CHAPTER

VIDEOTAPE POSTPRODUCTION

When all production has been completed and the pictures are recorded on videotape, the succeeding steps in the finishing of the commercial are called postproduction. Videotape postproduction consists of editing and mastering.

The equivalents of film opticals and answer prints are part of videotape editing. In this chapter we will also include distribution to stations, because most of today's duplicates are on videotape. Storage will also be covered because film and tape elements are usually stored together. In some cases film elements are dubbed to tape so they can be stored more conveniently.

Videotape editing is the process of arranging pieces of picture and sound information into a sequence that conforms to the commercial originally conceived by the writer and art director. Although the results of an electronic edit might be identical to a final film edit, they exist in two separate worlds of technology.

Film editing is a hands-on process; the editor's hands are in constant contact with the film, cutting, splicing,

viewing, marking, matching. Electronic editing is just the opposite; the tape editor might not even see the original tape as it is threaded on a tape deck in an equipment room some distance removed (Figure 7-1). The picture is only visible on the monitor after it has been routed through a multitude of various amplifiers, players, switchers, time-base correctors, time-code generators, and other electronic mysteries that are part of electronic editing.

The production breakthrough in electronic editing was the ability to record on videotape reference numbers that could be used for editing in the same manner as edge numbers on film. These recorded numbers, called a time code, were developed by the SMPTE and adopted as an American national standard (ANS 9812) in 1975.

The SMPTE time code is a digital code containing a continuous series of numbers that shows hours, minutes, second, and frames. It is usually recorded on one of the audio tracks or on a separate SMPTE track (Figure 7-2). The numbers can be recorded at the time of production or as a preliminary to postproduction. They maintain sync between separate players and recorders and are used on multichannel audio tracks for complex sound mixing. Depending on the type of video editing equipment, time-code numbers can be displayed on the picture monitor and on a computer data-display monitor and used for editing reference.

The big artistic breakthrough in videotape editing was development of the ability to view and control videotape one frame at a time. Frame-by-frame editing made electronic editing a precision craft for the first time.

The electronic breakthrough in editing probably came with the time-base corrector. This mysterious black box corrects minute flaws in the video signal on playback, so producers no longer fear the peculiar things that formerly happened at an electronic edit. The once-familiar picture rolling, horizontal instability, color shifts, and picture dropouts have been corrected through the use of this control, which automatically corrects any speed or signal variations as the image is transferred or edited. This is one of the few standardized pieces of equipment in the electronic recording field.

(Courtesy Editel-Chicago)

Figure 7-1. The master equipment room at Editel-Chicago. This room has every format of tape recorder and all necessary backup and support equipment to service editing suites and a studio.

Figure 7-2. The SMPTE time code placed on a picture monitor to establish an editing print.

EDITING

There are two broad classifications of videotape editing—on-line and off-line. With off-line the immediate result of the edit is a ¾-inch or a ½-inch helical-scan videotape of nonbroadcast quality. This edit is used for approval, and is later matched (conformed) either automatically or manually to the air-quality 1-inch or 2-inch master tape that can be duplicated for distribution. Helical scanning is common to small-format recorders; the magnetic signal is recorded diagonally rather than vertically as in 2-inch recordings. This is an oversimplified explanation, but sufficient for general purposes (Figure 7-3).

With on-line editing, all the elements used in the edit—and the tape that results from the editing session—are broadcast quality and can be used for duplication. On-line editing time is double the cost of off-line; if the edit-

ing session takes a great amount of time or if approval of the finished spot is uncertain, it is much more economical to use off-line. Another excellent reason for using off-line editing is availability of equipment. Broadcast-quality tape machines are necessary for all transfers (dubs) that are sent to the broadcasters. Tying these machines up for a long edit session is a cost and scheduling problem for the tape service.

Film editors are becoming familiar with off-line equipment, and more and more of them are handling the switcher themselves. The switcher is the master control panel through which all electronic cues are controlled. Many film-finishing services have added tape capabilities to their editing; although most of this is off-line, one-inch recorders are making it possible for them to become on-line as well.

Off-Line Editing

The first step in off-line editing is to transfer the original tape to ¾-inch cassettes with time coding. This means that in addition to the picture, the original air-quality 2-inch or 1-inch tape must have a digital signal placed on it that will read time and frame count and display it on the monitor screen when needed. The time code is the equivalent of edge numbers on film and is an accurate reference for all editing. There are a number of computer editing systems in use, but typical ones seem to be the CMX, developed by Columbia Broadcasting and Memorex, and Mach One, developed by Mach One Digital Systems, Inc.

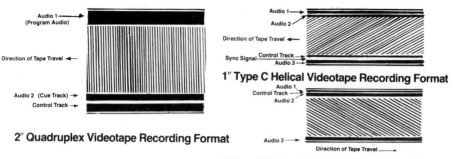

Audio 1 ⟶ (Program Audio)

Direction of Tape Travel ⟵

Audio 2 (Cue Track) ⟶
Control Track ⟶

2″ Quadruplex Videotape Recording Format

Audio 1 ⟶
Audio 2
Direction of Tape Travel ⟵
Sync Signal — Control Track ⟶
Audio 3 ⟶

1″ Type C Helical Videotape Recording Format

Audio 1
Control Track ⟶
Audio 2

Audio 3 ⟶
Direction of Tape Travel ⟶

1″ Type B Helical Videotape Recording Format

Figure 7-3. Videotape recording formats.

General handling of an edit is the same in both systems and represents the state of the art.

If only two recorders are on the edit chain—one for playing and one for recording—it is only possible to make cuts. At least three must be available for a simple television edit with dissolves and effects. Original tape is transferred to two cassettes with time-coding matching on all tapes. The first scene is located and the number on the time code noted where the editor wishes an effect to take place. The computer is instructed to actuate the main switcher with the selected effect when this number is reached. Instructions are also displayed on a computer display monitor (Figure 7-4). As the original tape is reviewed on the video monitor, other instructions are typed into the computer and displayed on the computer monitor. At any time it is possible to rehearse or review what has been set up on the computer without recording. A scene can be recorded on the master tape while editing, but as a rule sections are set up on the computer and reviewed be-

fore they are recorded. Search for selected takes or repeat of takes is greatly expedited by the fast forward and fast rewind available on most offline players and recorders; this feature is quite similar to the one on flat-bed film-editing console.

In any method of electronic editing, special effects are made by separate effects generators. There are many manufacturers of this equipment, and the sophistication of the effects are in direct ratio to the cost of the equipment (Figure 7-5). With computer programming, any available effects can be incorporated into an edit. Film effects are the basis for electronic ones, but a film optical that might take weeks to complete can be done in minutes on tape. Most important, the optical can be immediately checked on the monitor; there is no need to wait for a print from the lab. If the optical is not right, it can be redone at once.

Type can also be generated electronically, but the standard procedure for national TV spots is to supply an art card with reverse (white-on-black) type. An art director's trained taste in

Figure 7-4. Computer display monitor and keyboard being used in an off-line videotape edit.

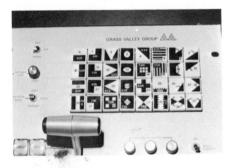

Figure 7-5. Programmed optical symbols on a Grass Valley switcher.

type design is far superior to the snap judgment of the electronic editor and supervisor. Type faces available in a type generator are usually limited and, of course, hand lettering is impossible. Colors, outlines, placement, and other variations can be added electronically from a reverse type card. A separate camera must be used to include the art card in the final edit.

Many off-line editorial systems do not have a full range of support equip-

ment, and small-format tapes must be ordered from an on-line service with a camera, full film chain, and broadcast-quality tape decks. Other off-line companies have complete equipment for all types of editing but prefer to do first edits in nonair tape format. In these cases, the only difference between the two systems is the type of tape recorder used. A good film chain has a 35-mm projector that runs forward, backward, and stops on a single frame; a 16-mm projector of top quality with the same capabilities; and a 35-mm double frame (two-by-two-inch) slide projector.

It is extremely important that an accurate log of time already used and projected time use be kept during editing. A spot that is one second too long after editing cannot be used on the air; it must be corrected before it goes to on-line.

On-Line Editing

The best reason for on-line editing is that tapes can be at the station the following day. A master videotape that results from an on-line edit is high-band broadcast quality and ready for duplicating and distribution. The editing is generally the same as in off-line but includes the availablity of broadcast-quality tape decks and probably a greater number of more sophisticated effects generators tied in to the switcher.

One of the additional operations is the use of a color-correction step. When original material is transferred to tape rolls used for editing, it is color-balanced so that each take looks right (Figure 7-6). The editor does not have color balance to contend with during the session. This correction is usually completed in a separate room with a colorist who specializes in this kind of work.

The newest development in videotape is complete one-inch postproduction. These are machines with many capabilities not available on the older, larger two-inch machines. Fast forward and search, freeze frame, superior quality, and compact size make them the videotape recorder of the future (Figure 7-7). Videotape recording equipment in on-line editing is usually in an area separated from the actual editing suite. This equipment room contains the film chain, insert and title cameras, VTRs, and banks of monitors. Communication from editor to technicians is usually on a headset or speaker system.

(Courtesy Editel-Chicago)

Figure 7-6. Videotape color correction and editing suite.

prefer to have the editor face the clients and only display the master monitor. Every company has different equipment and procedures (Figure 7-9). Film production with videotape finish is on-line and will be covered later in this section.

Many editing services, both on-line and off-line, have capabilities for storing the computer information of the final edit (Figure 7-10). This storage material varies from floppy disks to computer printouts and permits automatic recall and simple corrections of the final edit in a minimum amount of time. Maintaining quality through generations of duplication is much easier to do on videotape than on film. Recent tests have indicated that as many as ten generations of dubbings can be made from a master without any appreciable loss of quality, if the equipment is properly set up and maintained.

Figure 7-7. The RCA TR-800 one-inch type-C videotape recorder mounted in a studio console permits the use of many accessories.

Either editing method is very exciting to the director or production supervisor. The editing rooms, called suites, are always designed for the comfort of clients: large comfortable furniture, attractive subdued lighting, and a large color monitor for viewing the edit (Figure 7-8). Banks of small monitors used by the editor for cueing and scene selection are on view, and every move in editing can be followed by the clients, although some services

(Courtesy Editel-Chicago)

Figure 7-8. A videotape editing suite.

Figure 7-9. A computerized editing suite. *Left to right*: production switcher, digital video effects (DVE) generator, computer keyboard and monitor, audio player, character generator and monitor, and black-and-white camera for titles.

Figure 7-10. A computer keyboard and its monitor being used in videotape editing. The displayed time codes can be stored for future use.

SOUND EDITING

Sound editing is much more complicated on videotape than it is on film, particularly with synchronous sound. Videotape has sound recorded on an audio channel next to the video. To keep sound and picture in sync it is necessary to transfer both simultaneously to the master as the edit is made. After the complete edit, the audio track must be balanced and effects and music mixed. This means another transfer of sound track for balance and the setting up of additional audio channels for additional sound elements.

The facilities of the individual tape-editing service determine the method of mixing. Voice-over is fairly simple—the completely mixed audio track is put on the master videotape and the visuals are edited to match it. There are instances when the most practical production approach is to make a ¼-inch synchronous transfer from the videotape of the on-camera voice and then switch to magnetic perforated film and complete the sound as if it were a film track. This is then transferred to an audio track on the master videotape.

A videotape commercial has a second and a half more sound than a comparable film commercial. This is because videotape sound tracks are along the side of the picture signal

Figure 7-11. A new computerized audio editing room. *Left to right:* an eighteen-track in and twenty-four-track out computer audio mixer, SMPTE time-code synchronizer, twenty-four-track recorder, four-track recorder, and eight-track recorder.

Figure 7-12. Another view of the same studio mixing room. Notice the picture monitors using ¾-inch videotape players held in sync by time code, and the announcer's booth in the background.

whereas film sound is twenty-six frames ahead of the picture to allow for threading a projector and the relation of the picture aperture to the sound pickup head. Requirements for film prints specify a second and a half of silence at the start of each spot so the sound track is not cut if prints are spliced together. These added precious seconds of sound are another reason for videotape postproduction.

The complications of videotape audio editing are the main reason for using an additional ¼-inch recorder on the set for sound only. With the audio man keeping an accurate log, this backup recorder could save time in a video edit, particularly when on-set sound effects and off-camera voices are needed.

The newest method of sound editing is to use a 2-inch multichannel tape recorder and rerecord all synchronous sound takes with the time code from the picture as a guide (Figures 7-11 and 7-12). The magnetic sound tracks are then balanced, mixed, and placed in their proper position (relative to the final videotape picture edit) by computer as in a standard off-line edit; ¾-inch tape is used for picture reference during sound mixing. When the sound mix has been completed and approved, the off-line computer time-code numbers go on-line for dubbing to the master videotape. Only time will tell whether this procedure will become standard.

ELECTRONIC ANIMATION (COMPUTER GRAPHICS)

Electronic animation is an exclusive outgrowth of modern television hardware. Video images are created and regulated by computer controls on amplifiers and signal generators. From static artwork, video animation can make gears spin, legs move, logos vibrate, and create many other types of movement that are associated with traditional ink and paint animation.

There are two different systems of producing electronic video graphics. The original one uses a continuous signal known as analog and distorts this signal through a series of generators and controls until the resulting picture on the monitor has the desired movement and configuration. This animation can be created in real time (the actual time the equipment is operated), and changes or corrections can be made immediately. When imagery on the monitor has been approved, it can be videotaped for editing or filmed to be integrated into a film commercial. Some companies that specialize in this type of video graphics have equipment that can generate more

than television's standard 525 scan lines in order to achieve excellent definition in film production.

The newer system converts the analog signal into a digital one. While the analog signal is continuous, the digital signal is made of bits of information that can be handled and stored by a computer. The computer solves problems given to it and places the answer on a video monitor; once on the monitor, the information can be repeated and recorded in the manner needed. An illustration of this capability is the electronic making of the "in-betweens" for drawn extremes in an animated commercial: the computer is told to go from position A to position B in eighteen frames with the same style of graphics. The computer does this and shows the complete sequence on the monitor; if approved, the solution is then recorded. The computer also has a memory capability, and complete sequences of computer-generated animation can be played and recorded. The savings in time and money can be very substantial in many projects. It is possible to have the computer solve the problem of graphically turning a picture of an attractive woman into something as mundane as a bar of soap. The potential of this digital hardware is limitless.

This type of animation is expected to become very popular as computers become cheaper and easier to operate. The mixing of live and computer images will become commonplace as this combination develops. There is a confusion between the words used to describe electronic animation and standard animation photographed on a computer-controlled animation stand; both methods are called computer animation, but they are entirely different types of production (see the section on animation in Chapter 5, pages 91–99).

FILM FINISHED ON VIDEOTAPE

The use of videotape for finishing commercials originally photographed on film has increased tremendously in the last few years. There are a number of reasons for this growth: it saves a great deal of money and time in postproduction; videotape's magnetic sound track is far superior to film's optical sound track; many generations of intermediate film steps can be bypassed, increasing quality; and videotape color correction allows a great deal of control over the duplicates that are sent to the television stations for broadcasting.

A 1980 survey indicates that 75 percent of nonlocal spot production is shot on film, and 70 percent of the finish is on tape. Tape finish of filmed commercials is generally completed in one of three ways.

Approved 35-mm or 16-mm silent answer prints can be transferred to a master videotape at the same time as the original master magnetic mix. There is a slight time saving over film with this procedure, but the greatest benefit is high sound quality and absence of dirt and abrasions on the picture. It is a simple matter to produce subsequent film prints, since all the expensive optical work has been completed and an optical track negative is all that is needed. This system is ideal for network commercials because of quality demands and limited distribution. Tape dubs are much more expensive than 16-mm prints. The cost of this type of videotape finish is minimal at the electronic level; the control is excellent.

The most common method of film-to-tape finish is the A-and-B-roll system (Figure 7-13). The approved work print is used as a reference for making up two rolls of color-corrected work print called A and B rolls. Each roll contains alternating scenes that overlap. The two rolls are transferred to separate videotape machines on a film chain. The editing is completed by combining the two rolls as they are rerecorded on a third machine. All the effects on the switcher or control panel can be incorporated as a computer automatically switches from one

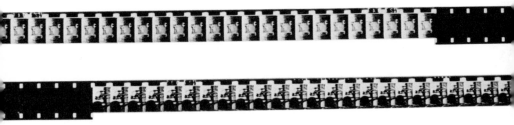

Figure 7-13. A- and B-roll overlap prepared for videotape transfer and editing.

roll to the other. Switching can be made on a frame. This method is an excellent time saver, and, if no film prints are needed, can also be a money saver.

The third approach is to do all the editing on tape. This means transferring prints of the approved and color-timed film takes and handling them as if they were from an original videotape production. Another recent method of film-to-tape transferring with great potential involves the use of a piece of equipment called a flying spot scanner and permits an original camera negative to be used in transferring to

Figure 7-14. The Rank Cinetal flying-spot scanner, used for transferring film to videotape.

videotape. In this procedure the positive film print is completely eliminated. A flying spot scanner must be used for this step because the normal intermittent action of a projector in a film chain might scratch the fragile negative (Figure 7-14). Quality is superb, but many producers are concerned about damage in handling the original negative. The scanner replaces the film chain as it can make broadcast-quality videotape from any type of film—16-mm, 35-mm, positive, or negative.

The only drawbacks to this method are the loss of random-access editing and the necessity of making immediate editing decisions. The hourly cost of electronic editing is five times the cost of film editing. However, the savings in time and optical and lab costs could very well compensate for the additional cost.

VIDEOTAPE-TO-FILM TRANSFERS

Videotape gives maximum quality to electronic recording and reproduction. The magnetic signals that are stored on tape can only be viewed on an electronic monitor, but there are occasions when viewing pictures on a television monitor is not practical, and on these occasions film projection is the answer. The need for a videotape-to-film transfer is evident in large-audience situations, where television commercials must be shown to a sales force; in retail point-of-purchase, where only 8-mm projectors are available; and in special television distribution. The best transfers are not as good as original film or original videotape.

There are three general types of transfers avilable; each demands excellent original-picture quality. The lowest-cost transfer system is the kinescope, a motion-picture camera with a special shutter that photographs the face of a television tube. This system is adequate for a record of the videotape content but yields a relatively poor quality print.

A second process, electron-beam recording, takes the electronic signal from the tape and deposits it directly on film. It requires a near-perfect signal and superior equipment and technicians to deliver good quality.

The third and most expensive system involves computer enhancement of the video signal. This is called tweaking the signal. Again, a perfect signal is needed as the built-in limitations of the electronic chain are added to film's chemical limitations. Although the combination of the two recordings is not quite as good as either one of them, videotape-to-film transfers are common.

CLOSED CAPTIONING FOR THE HEARING IMPAIRED

Closed captioning is a television service created for the more than 14 million hearing-impaired Americans who have difficulty understanding the audio on programs and commercials. A special symbol identifies these programs (Figure 7-15). The captioning starts after the commercial is completed and a master tape is available. A ¾-inch and 2-inch time-coded cassette and script are sent to the National Captioning Institute, where the original audio is condensed into cap-

tions that can be easily read. These captions are edited to audio time and stored in a computerized system that is able to place the code on the master tape. When a closed-captioned program is broadcast, TV sets with an adapter or a built-in decoder are able to see an approximation of the dialogue or commentary (Figure 7-16).

Figure 7-15. This symbol designates programs that have been closed-captioned for the hearing impaired.

(Courtesy National Captioning Institute, Inc.)

Figure 7-16. A closed-captioned television picture as it appears on a television set with a decoder.

DISTRIBUTION

The motivation behind television-commercial production is to broadcast a finished commercial that induces the viewer to purchase the product or service. Videotape or film production is only a step in broadcast advertising. The finished commercial must be sent to the broadcast-origination station for broadcast—it must be distributed. There is considerably more to distribution than the shipping of prints to stations. Many advertising agencies work through specialized distribution companies because of the amount of material that must be handled and the specialized services needed. The distribution service is the final checkpoint before the film or tape is broadcast; it can also become a single-agency source for print or tape procurement, reeling, boxing, checking, shipping, and guaranteeing the completed spot's arrival at its final destination.

Either film prints or videotapes are acceptable for use on the air. Film prints are considerably cheaper, but videotape does not scratch and has better quality. Also, stations will generally transfer to tape anything sent them for broadcasting. Pete Markovich, a vice-president of MGS, one of the country's largest distribution organizations, says that more than 80 percent of all commercials are now distributed on videotape, and within a few years he expects it to be close to 100 percent. Because of volume purchasing, the cost of prints and dubbings is usually no more expensive at a distribution company than through a videotape service or laboratory. Small quantities of duplicates for spot buys can usually be purchased from the postproduction service and shipped by the agency to the station.

When the advertising agency has approved the answer print or videotape master, all printing elements and master videotape material is sent to the distribution company. The agency's traffic department then informs the distribution company of the broadcast schedule. Quantity prints and videotapes are ordered; each one is reeled, boxed, titled with its approved title, and coded with its proper number. Each order is spot-checked by an inspector to make sure that it is the proper commercial and that the quality matches the approved material. There are many horror stories about print distribution when time has not permitted a proper checking of the material. One personal experience had to do with a network commercial that was made for Seven-Up, and which ran nationwide with a Dr Pepper sound track. This spot had been approved by the laboratory, studio, network clearance, network programming, and agency traffic—it can happen!

If prints or videotape dubs are not spot-checked by traffic or production, the following types of irregularities can occur:

1. Scratches
2. Bad color
3. Poor sound
4. No sound
5. Incorrect sound
6. Picture out of frame
7. Tape noise
8. Tape roll (picture instability)
9. Tape banding (picture shows different bands)
10. Tape dropout

From a shipping list or labels supplied by the agency's traffic or business department, the distribution company labels and ships film or tape to the stations in a method guaranteed to get it there on time. The guarantee is possible because any reputable distribution company is insured against mishaps in shipping or even against errors of omission. If a mistake on its part causes a missed air date, the insurance reimburses all parties for air time and expenses. If necessary, a letter of instruction can also accompany the print or dub.

This procedure is necessary only if distribution is nationwide and many productions are concurrent; local commercials or limited-market commercials are no problem for either an agency or producer and can be handled in postproduction without the use of a distribution service. The latest method of distribution to stations is by satellite. Time is purchased on a commercial satellite and the station or distribution-company branch is notified of the broadcast time. The broadcast is picked up, videotaped and is immediately ready for use. There are still a number of bugs in this system, but it may well be the method of the future.

STORAGE

Storage of production materials is recognized as a major problem in the television-commercial industry. Much of the problem is created because no one wants to throw out something that costs a lot of money. Procrastination seems to be the order of the day, and the boxes keep piling up. When a film or videotape commercial has been completed, the material used to produce it is usually reeled, canned, boxed, and put in a carton. Each spot usually means about twenty twelve-inch cans of 35-mm film or six twelve-inch boxes of videotape. The film cans contain negative, work print, work-print trims, NG takes, sound tracks, mixing elements, intermediate positives, optical elements, and the printing material; the videotape boxes contain mastering elements and original tape.

Distribution companies, production companies, and laboratories usually file and keep printing elements and production elements for six months after the production date; after this period of time, disposition should be made. This applies to either film or videotape. Film-printing material is usually kept for years; but the permanence of color in TV-commercial film prints and negatives is now a production consideration. The color in a standard film print noticeably deteriorates in three to four years, and the color negative begins to degrade a few years later. Videotape is still being studied. Deterioration is another factor to consider when decisions about storage are made.

Too many advertising agencies ignore the storage problem. Production companies can be very lax in returning production elements, and many times the elements become scattered because clients change, production houses change, and a variety of optical houses and laboratories are used. A storage company is very pleased to gather up all this material and store it in their vaults for a monthly charge based on the number of individual cans; there is also an inventory charge. Although monthly charges vary between fifteen and twenty-five cents per can, it adds up. An active advertising agency might pay thousands of dollars every month within a short period of time.

There are a number of solutions to this problem. The agency can destroy all material except printing elements after approval. This is dangerous because of future corrections and the use of old material in other commercials. Or, the agency can destroy everything except printing elements and original, and review the material annually for possible reuse. A third possibility is to make a one-inch videotape master of retained elements and destroy the film original. This has a higher initial expense, but the number of cans is minimal. Of course, the agency is always legally covered if their client gives them a written order to destroy all elements of a commercial.

CHAPTER

OPPORTUNITIES AND THE FUTURE

Sponsored television is one of the most cost-effective methods of advertising available, and there are no indications that this will change in the future. The time for a thirty-second spot on the Super Bowl may cost $250,000, but since 100 million people view it, the cost per viewer is only a quarter of a cent. This extremely expensive time buy has a lower per-viewer cost than magazine or newspaper space, and television advertising has the added value of being both audible and visible.

The home video recorder has been seen as a threat to network advertisers; but, although it may reduce the numbers of immediate viewers, the recording of programs (and commercials) ensures repeat viewing, which can benefit the advertiser. Prerecorded programs on video cassettes and video discs are more apt to affect the motion-picture box office than sponsored television because, as in theaters, there is a payment associated with viewing; it is not free.

How does a newcomer enter the field of television advertising? To begin, since all advertising centers around the advertising agency, this is the best point of employment breakthrough. At the account level (account service and account executive), a college education and a degree in advertising seem to be musts. Large agencies still recruit account people from graduate programs at good universities. A business-administration background is particularly helpful in an advertising agency in broadcast management; and, of course, lawyers are always necessary.

Advertising agencies need writers more than any other group. However, they always seem to be looking for experienced ones. A journalism education is a tremendous advantage and many of the agency creative directors I know came out of journalism school. They initially wrote anything that was available—classified ads, local papers, trade papers, articles, whatever they could find; it is all experience. Once in the advertising fraternity, everything is a matter of timing and keeping an ear to the ground.

Industrial writing is closely allied to advertising writing and offers many opportunities to gain experience.

Large companies have internal-communication media that demand writers. There are also brochures, sales meetings, industrial films, and videotapes for in-house production. Experience and personal contacts (who you know) increase.

The team of writer and art director is the base of all ad-agency creativity. The two are always in the driver's seat in television-commercial production. An art background is very important in the business of making television commercials; in any phase of production, it is important to have a knowledge of fashion, architecture, design, and type styles. Good art schools give some of this background, and it is still possible to apprentice for established artists or studios. The ability to draw opens up the field of storyboard preparation. Sample storyboards are extremely useful, and to get them might require doing some storyboards for small agencies on speculation (no pay). It is not easy, but it is a lot better to make the round of agencies with samples than without them.

Letters to advertising agencies enclosing a resume should be sent. Most libraries have a directory of advertising agencies that lists departments and clients. Write a letter to the head of the department that interests you in a number of agencies. Many times this letter will be given over to a personnel manager, but you will have made an extra contact. Keep your eyes open when reading the business section of the daily newspaper. When an agency has recently landed a new account, it is usually looking for help. The library is also a source for the trade journals; *Advertising Age, Television Age,* and local publications have classified ads and news stories that will give some tips. Getting a job in commercial broadcasting is like any type of selling; first there is prospecting, then making the presentation, and finally, closing the sale.

Another specialty in the advertising agency is the television producer. Most people hired as producers are experienced, and it is not unusual for established producers to move from agency to agency with an increase in salary. A good producer can also move into a production company as a manager, representative, or director. My experience indicates that, in general, producers are promoted from within an agency, men and women in about equal numbers (most executive producers are men because they started more than ten years ago). Producers promoted from within an agency were secretaries, receptionists, junior writers, new artists, researchers, or even traffic managers. Below the producer position there is usually a training step called an assistant producer or a production assistant. The duties in this learning position usually include calling for sample reels, setting up screenings, arranging auditions, attending production meetings and taking production notes, and helping with the volume of paperwork that seems to grow every day.

One of the reasons that producers can be trained more rapidly than in former years is that technical knowledge and experience have become less important than administrative ability and personality. Now there are a number of people who share production responsibility. In this book I have used the titles producer and agency supervisor interchangeably. With equipment such as the video assist on the film camera and videotape cameras, a scene can be viewed immediately and a writer or art director can give an immediate approval. This authority could make one of them the agency supervisor. All advertising agencies vary in organization.

There are many opportunities in a production studio for someone who has an interest in television-commercial production. The nontechnical areas need one approach, the technical areas another. Many advertising-agency employees become members of a production studio, and production-company employees sometimes end up working for an agency. This is particularly noticeable with directors. An agency art director who has had a considerable amount of experience working on commercial production and has supervised still photography has a good potential as a director. This is especially true if the art director has worked for a number of agencies and is more than a storyboard renderer. A formal education in communication, broadcasting, and film also gives a good base for a career in television-commercial production.

The job that gives the greatest opportunity for the beginner is production assistant. This is initially a low-paying, "gofer" type of work (you "go for" this and "go for" that). The studio's production manager usually employs a number of production assistants on a job to help in casting, go for props, pick up wardrobe, find locations, handle releases, pick up and arrange transportation, take care of catering, duplicate scripts, and do a multitude of other chores. Since a new production assistant is much cheaper than a member of one of the trade unions, there are times when conflicts appear at a production company because of union contracts with studio mechanics, property people, makeup and hairdressing, and wardrobe people. In a nonunion company a production assistant can do everything; much of the work performed by a production assistant overlaps that of an assistant director. This is a problem in some companies. Although most production assistants would like to become assistant directors, DGA assistant directors do not usually have any desire to become directors. In the DGA, an assistant director is a profession.

This seems the proper place to examine the union stituation among commercial production companies. It is a fairly complicated issue. The areas of the country where union membership is an important consideration are New York, Chicago, Los Angeles, and, to a much lesser degree, San Francisco, Phoenix, Miami, St. Louis, Detroit, and Washington, D.C. All other areas are not union-oriented, and most production of commercials is nonunion. Most of the unions in the industry are offshoots of motion-picture production or television broadcasting. The International Alliance of Theatrical and Stage Employees (IATSE) was originally a theatrical union and now represents cameramen, editors, laboratory workers, electricians, gaffers, and sound technicians, among other trades. You must be a member of the IATSE to get employment in a contract company. To become a member you must present your application to the board of directors of the specific local and be approved.

If the applicant is accepted, it is sometimes necessary to serve some form of apprenticeship, at a very low rate of pay, until proficiency is established. A person applying for an assistant-camera card would probably apprentice for at least a year before being accepted. Once accepted as an assistant cameraman it is possible to become a camera operator, a cameraman, and ultimately a director of photography on features and program production. Editors, laboratory workers, and stagehands seem to be in plentiful supply within the union; but if a person makes a reputation in a non-union capacity, the union is usually happy to grant a card. The "who you know" element is important in becoming a union member; the IATSE is a somewhat closed union that has a loose form of hiring hall. Employers can call the union office and ask for workers by name or occupation, or they can call workers directly. Videotape crews are frequently mixed, meaning that different unions and even nonunion workers are combined.

Another union that represents television network employees and some film technicians is the National Association of Broadcast Employees and Technicians (NABET). Originated at NBC in 1934, it is a younger union than the IATSE and is only concerned with broadcast and its associated industries. Anyone employed in the broadcast business can join NABET. There are dues, working conditions, and minimum pay scales, as in any union.

The Directors Guild of America (DGA) is also active in representing TV-commercial-production-company employees. The guild also represents assistant directors. It was organized to represent motion-picture directors and now represents every type of film and tape director. To become a director member, a director needs a job as a director, pays the initiation fee and dues, and agrees to work only with companies that are signatories to the DGA contract. The rates for minimum pay, working conditions, and producer contributions to pension, health and welfare funds are excellent, so most recognized commercial directors belong to the guild. Becoming a director is usually a long-term project; an agency background as an art director, advertising photographer, and producer have been the springboard for many successful directors.

Many directors also become cameramen. They usually develop this ability slowly, working with experienced motion-picture cameramen and assistants. Initially they only operate the camera, following the action and composing the pictures in the eyepiece as the camera technicians set the aperture and take care of all the mechanics. As the director gains experience and feels competent on the camera, the unions may accept him or her as a cameraman. The TV-commercial director-cameraman rarely works on features or programs because of limited technical background.

The assistant director has another method of obtaining membership: in Los Angeles and New York, a DGA office has been established to supervise an assistant-directors training program. Applications are accepted by this office, and some applicants are chosen to participate in the program. They are paid a salary and sent out on jobs with regular assistant directors. After about a year of working they are given full status and made accessible to the industry by being placed on the availability list.

A method of obtaining membership in other areas is to be requested by a signatory company. As long as someone is employed by the signatory, he or she is classified as a provisional assistant director. When sufficient time (between one and two years) has accumulated in the performance of this work, the provisional classification is dropped and full assistant-director status given. A DGA member is not permitted to work for a nonsignatory company, and this restriction can reduce the amount of available work. Producing television commercials is a very competitive business, and the nonunion companies rarely have any employee benfits. There are many excellent production companies—some union, some nonunion, some mixed.

Another production-studio position available to newcomers is representing a director and studio to the advertising agencies. This is a sales job and takes a special personality. Calling on advertising agencies with sample reels, setting up meetings, taking buy-ers to lunch, smiling a lot, and being nice to people that you don't particularly like are all part of this job. Some people enjoy it and are very successful, with a minimum of production knowledge. It usually pays a commission plus expenses.

The nontechnical requirements in videotape production are the same as for film. Within the full-service videotape companies, there are very few staff DGA directors and assistants and not a great number of other union employees because union jurisdictions have not yet been established. Many people would like to get into the videotape business because it is new and seems to have a more exciting future than film. The only new part of videotape commercial production is the equipment, and there is a tremendous call for electronics experts to operate and maintain it.

A degree in electrical engineering is a great asset in the videotape field. Knowing why and how things work is very valuable. An aptitude for computer programming expedites electronic editing, although the editing principles are those of film. Working as a technician with film editors helps obtain this knowledge. A lighting director has a responsibility comparable to the stage lighting designer, and in television commercials is sometimes replaced by a cameraman. Because almost all commercials are produced in cinematic (one-camera) style with editing of separate takes, film people are expanding into the videotape industry as directors, cameramen, and editors.

Sound engineers are electrical specialists, and sound mixers, on the floor and in the studio, are artists. The problem of making good clean sound in difficult situations is identical on film and videotape. Videotape sound is recorded on the picture material. The microphoning, characteristics, and reproduction of sound can make or break a production—the job takes a lot of experience. Studio mixing is even more difficult than floor mixing and calls for more artistry. A voice-over narration is fairly simple, but recording a music track on twenty-four channels takes a specialist. It is the same talent that is needed to record albums, with the additional problem of videotape and broadcasting limitations.

Finding a job in the sound industry usually means getting into a sound studio and working as a "gofer" or dubbing technician, making points in every job. I also know successful sound engineers who were self-taught and loved music, sounds, hi-fi, and reproducing sound. The videotape sound engineer combines all the above requirements with computer-programming ability.

Electronics trade schools can help someone interested in videotape. Videotape technicians will never lose their identity because knowledge of electronic equipment is the most important contribution to videotape accomplishments. When video engineers make the equipment simple enough, the film specialist will be able to use it, but there is no reason that the video technician cannot learn film techniques and remain in control.

The future of television commercials seems to be in pay television. Originally planned as noncommercial broadcasting, cable and satellite television, in today's economics, need commercial sponsorship. Many subscription channels are picking up standard commercial broadcasting from stations using satellites; but with the new contracts negotiated by the SAG, DGA, and Writers Guild, it appears that some type of program sponsorship will be necessary even on the cable networks. Although the rules of public broadcasting do not apply to cable TV, the production techniques of the commercials are the same.

Television commercials are here to stay. The percentages may change, but they will continue to be produced on film and on videotape. Motion pictures have been in their same basic form for fifty years; the chances for any major change or breakthrough is small. Videotape has been in use for twenty-five years, but space-age technology has been the catalyst for the enormous advances of recent years. Each passing week brings new developments in design and operation of videotape equipment. For the television commercial producer, director, cameraman, editor, and technicians, the tools of television production are becoming more advanced; it will be interesting to see if creative people can keep up with them.

GLOSSARY

A & B roll: Two separate rolls of film or videotape that are integrated in postproduction.

ABC: American Broadcasting Company, a national television network.

Account executive: An advertising agency employee with the primary responsibility of contacting and servicing the account (client).

ADR: Automatic dialogue replacement. A computer-assisted method of postdubbing sound.

Affiliate: Television station associated by contract with a national network.

AFTRA: American Federation of Radio and Television Artists. A union representing radio and videotape performers.

AF of M: American Federation of Musicians. A union representing musicians in the broadcast industry.

Agency commission: The 15 percent discount given to advertising agencies when they purchase time or space.

AICP: Association of Independent Commercial Producers. The bid form set up by this association has become the industry standard.

Air check: Checking the broadcast quality of commercials for the client or advertising agency. Radio air checks have been quite successful, but television air checks are still difficult to record.

Amplifier: Device for increasing power, usually used in connection with an electric signal.

Animatic: A rough presentation of a television commercial; from the name of a 16-mm slide projector formerly used in presentations.

Animation: The process by which individual drawings are photographed one frame at a time with movement changes in each separate drawing; when projected at twenty-four frames per second, the movement seems lifelike. It also applies to any static object that can be made to move through single-frame or stop-motion photography.

Animation stand: Sophisticated motion picture copy stand used for photographing titles or animation.

Answer print: The first fully corrected composite (picture and sound) print made from a printing negative.

Aperture: The lens opening which determines the amount of light permitted to pass through a lens onto the recording surface.

APO: Action print only. An untimed silent print from an optical negative. Also called slop print.

Art director: The advertising agency supervisor of the artwork produced for advertising. A TV art director is concerned mainly with storyboards.

Aspect ratio: The relationship of the height of a picture to its width. The ratio in television is 3:4, in motion pictures 1:1.33.

Assistant director: A classification made by the Directors Guild. On television commercials, the job's main duty is taking administrative responsibilities from the director and coordinating activities of crew and performers.

Audio: Sound.

Base: The transparent acetate or mylar material on which an emulsion is supported. The shiny side of film.

Baby: A small spotlight, usually 750 watts.

Back light: Illumination of the subject from the rear. This often serves to separate the subject from the background by giving it a light edge.

Back-to-back: Commercials for programs that are adjacently broadcast.

Banding: The horizontal bands on a television picture.

Beam splitter: Device for splitting the beam of light being focused from a lens into more than one focal plane. Particularly useful in video assist and other camera viewing systems.

Billboard: Credits at the opening or closing of a program that list the sponsors.

Blue-screen process: A method of making a traveling matte on an optical bench. A cobalt-blue background is filtered out and becomes a high-contrast matte.

Boom: A movable beam that can extend a microphone over a set to pick up actors' voices.

Breakdown: The listing of all of the elements in a script that can affect production.

Bug-eye: An extremely wide-angle lens that distorts the picture and has a universal focus.

Burn out: A television picture that lacks tonal gradation in the light areas, usually indicating an equipment or lighting problem.

Cable television: The transmitting of a television signal through cables rather than over air waves. This method of transmission is not currently regulated by the FCC.

Camera operator: A cameraman concerned solely with operating the camera, with responsibility for camera moves, composition, focus, but not lighting.

Camera report: A report kept by the assistant cameraman that lists all scenes, takes, print takes, and any special information that might be of use to the laboratory.

Casting: Auditioning performers to select the cast.

Cassette: Self-contained reel of videotape that can be inserted in a VCR for viewing; available in ¾-inch, ½-inch, and ¼-inch widths.

CATV: Cable television.

CBS: Columbia Broadcasting System, a national television network.

C mount: A 16-mm threaded lens mount.

CCU: A video camera-control unit that makes remote corrections in color, focus, lens aperture, and contrast.

Cell: A clear acetate film used for animation; the name is derived from the cellophane originally used. Artwork drawn on this material is photographed one frame at a time on an animation stand.

Character design: The style of figure drawing in an animated commercial.

Character generator: A video generator with a selection of type faces that puts type characters on the screen.

Check print: Any print from a film negative used to check content and quality.

Click track: Rough sound track with clicks scratched in it for cueing voices. Used in post-dubbing.

Clio: An award given for commercials by the National Television Commercial Festival in New York.

Closed-circuit television: Nonbroadcast television that uses direct lines to selected sets; cable television is an example.

Code generator: A generator module that puts an identification code onto a videotape. The SMPTE number code recorded on the videotape shows hours, minutes, seconds, and frames.

Color meter: A hand-held instrument that can measure the color temperature of light.

Color temperature: The temperature of different wavelengths of light; red is low and blue is high. Incandescent light is approximately 3,200 degrees Kelvin, daylight about 5,400 degrees Kelvin.

Composite print: Film print containing both picture and sound.

Computer animation: Computer-controlled animation equipment or computer-generator graphics that are programmed to move.

Conform: Matching negative or print material to an edited work print.

Console: Control panel for sound and picture, containing monitors, switchers, and a variety of other controls.

Continuity clearance: Network or station department that checks legality of proposed commercial.

Contrast filter: A filter placed over the camera lens while photographing to reduce contrast. Available in a variety of degrees, it is frequently used for a cosmetic or high-key effect.

Control room: The room where engineering controls are located and, since it is isolated from the sound studio, where verbal commands can be given.

Cost plus: A type of bid that establishes a markup which further costs do not increase.

Countdown: The marked time built into a tape or film immediately preceding the picture and sound; it is used for cueing.

Crane: Large boom arm that carries camera and part of the crew; it moves up and down and also can dolly.

Crawl: Titles that slowly move up the screen and disappear at the top.

Creative director: Advertising-agency executive with responsibility for creating and executing advertising concepts.

CRI: Color reversal intermediate, a laboratory procedure for making duplicate negatives without making an intermediate positive.

Crystal control: A timing oscillator that gives accurate pulses to a camera motor to keep it at a constant speed. It can also be used to stabilize a television signal.

Cucaloris ("cookie"): An opaque flag on a stand with a pattern of holes cut in it to break up the light from a spotlight and cast a random pattern on a surface.

Cue card: A card placed off camera to prompt an on-camera performer; also called an idiot card.

Cue track: The area reserved on videotape for information other than audio and video signals.

Cut: An edited work print. A first cut would be the initial edit presented for approval.

Cutter: An opaque object used to cut off light from a particular area.

Cycle: In animation, a complete action that can be repeated.

Dailies: The first print of a newly developed negative from the previous day's shooting; same as rushes and work print.

Dealer spot: A television commercial made by a manufacturer to use in a local market as a wild spot. It usually has special video at the end so the dealer can drop in the local identification.

Decoder: A device on the TV receiver that separates captions from the standard picture signal and places them on the screen, referred to as closed captioning for the hearing impaired.

Definition: Clarity of picture; sharpness or resolution of image. On television, definition is determined by the number of scan lines.

Degradation: Deterioration of image quality.

Demographic characteristics: The age, gender, education, ethnicity, and economic characteristics of a population.

Digital recording: The recording of bits of information rather than a continuous signal (analog). Newest method of recording sound and video.

DGA: Directors Guild of America, a union representing motion picture and television directors.

Diffusion filters: Filters placed over the camera lens to soften sharp images; frequently used to glamorize women.

Dinky: Small spotlight of not over 250 watts.

Direct response advertising: Television advertising that results in phone or mail orders.

Director of photography: A film lighting director and head photographer of theatrical and program production.

Dissolve: Optically overlapping a fade-out and a fade-in on the same piece of film; a time-transition optical.

Documentary: Commercial purporting to show real life rather than staged scenes.

Dolly: A wheeled camera platform that can follow action or move for dramatic effect.

Double exposure: The combination of superimposed images on one piece of film. This can be done in original photography, on an optical bench, or in a laboratory.

Double system: A system of recording picture and sound on two separate strands of film.

Drop: A large painting used as a background, primarily to give depth to a set.

Dropout: A lack of tape information that usually shows up on the monitor as small white streaks. Poor tape is a common reason for this defect.

Dubbing: A magnetic duplicate made from an original master.

Edge numbers: Sometimes called key numbers, the print-through numbers marked by a manufacturer on each foot of film, making it easy to match negative to print.

Editing: Selecting, cutting, splicing, and arranging the many scenes in a production to arrive at its final form.

Effect: An artificially created impression. Visual effects are usually produced in the laboratory, on an optical bench, or through an electronic effects generator.

Effects bank: The part of a switcher that incorporates special effects into a video image.

Effects track: A sound track that carries wild (nonsync) sound effects, such as footsteps, doors closing, car noises.

EFP: Electronic field production, the highly portable, broadcast-quality small cameras that are used with one-inch or two-inch tape recorders.

Electron-beam recording: A method of making tape-to-film transfers. Much superior to the kinescope, this procedure makes a good-quality motion picture from a broadcast-quality videotape.

Electronic editing: Combining picture and sound elements without physically cutting them. A computer usually controls an electronic edit after it has been programmed by an editor.

Emulsion: A gelatin layer coated on an acetate base or support that contains a photosensitive material.

Enhancement: The electronic accentuation of color, contrast, definition, or any other desirable addition to an original recording.

ENG: Electronic news gathering, a small portable video camera chain with ¾-inch tape recorder.

Exposure meter: A small hand-held device that measures the amount of light.

Extra: A performer in a commercial who is not directly involved with the product; he or she is usually unrecognizable in the background.

Fax: An expression used by electronics specialists to mean that the facilities are available; the equivalent of "Camera is ready" on a film set.

FCC: Federal Communications Commission, a federal regulatory agency concerned with public communication.

Fill light: Light directed into shadows to soften contrast.

Film chain: An assortment of projection equipment arranged so the projected images can be picked up electronically.

Film gate: A part of the camera or projector mechanism that holds the film frame in position as it is exposed or projected.

Film stock: The type of raw stock used in production: black and white, reversal, color negative, 35-mm or 16-mm gauge.

Film transfer: A film copy of a videotape original.

Fishpole: A hand-held mike boom about the size of a fishpole.

Flag: An opaque material that is usually mounted on a standard used to block out unwanted light.

Flip: A film or electronic effect in which the picture turns completely around.

Flying spot scanner: A device that transfers a picture from film to videotape without projectors by continuously scanning the moving film with an electron beam.

Focal length: The length of the lens, which determines the size of the picture area.

Focus puller: The assistant cameraman, with a primary responsibility of adjusting the lens and keeping the picture in focus; a term used mostly with English crews.

Fog filter: A filter placed over a lens that gives the approximate look of overall fog.

Follow focus: Continuously changing the focus during shooting, as the lens-to-subject distance changes.

Foot candles: A measurement of light based on the amount of light given off by a candle at a one-foot distance.

Frame: A single picture on a strip of film.

Frames per second: The number of frames that pass through a camera or projector in one second; standard sound projection is 24 fps.

Free-lance: Not permanently employed; available on a job-to-job basis. A very common condition in the commercial-production industry.

Freeze-frame: Holding one frame so a scene appears to stop; sometimes called a stop or hold frame.

Friction head: Tripod head which uses sliding friction to assure smoothness of camera movement.

Gaffer: The chief electrician of a production crew; works closely on lighting with cameraman.

Generation: A step in duplication. The master is the first generation, a dubbing from the master is the second generation, a copy of the second generation is a third generation.

Generator: Motor-driven source of electrical power, frequently used on location.

Gobo: Opaque material used on an adjustable stand to block light.

Grain: The small particles of silver halides in a film emulsion that make up the image. Over-development or extreme enlargement give a grainy look to a picture.

Grip: A stagehand who moves scenery and handles equipment.

Gyroscope stabilizers: Small motors that stabilize action and smooth out movement, sometimes attached to cameras to assure even camera action.

Helical scan: A method of videotaping by which the signal is recorded with a diagonal rather than a vertical pattern. This method is used in the smaller-width videotapes.

Hidden camera: A production technique in which the subject being photographed is unaware of the camera.

High-contrast: A film with no middletones, just black and white. Usually refers to film used in optical matte procedures.

High-definition television: A doubling of the number of scan lines in video transmission and recording, to increase reception quality.

High hat: A very low camera support.

High-key: A type of lighting that produces a picture with the bulk of its color gradations between white and gray.

High-speed: Photography taken at a higher number of frames per second than projection speed.

HMI light: Hydrargyrum medium iodide light with a very high electrical efficiency. It has daylight color and a good range of wattages, and seems to be replacing arc lights for daylight location shooting.

Holding fee: A residual payment to performers if the TV spot is not broadcast.

IATSE: International Alliance of Theatrical and Stage Employees, a union of theater and motion-picture workers.

IBEW: International Brotherhood of Electrical Workers, one of the broadcast engineering unions.

In-betweens: Animation drawings that fill in the gaps between the extremes, or most significant actions, of a movement.

Insert: Closeups of products or people used to accentuate action, smooth out editing, or glamorize product.

Intercut: Cutting from one independent sequence of action to another to create a relation between the two.

Interlock: A system of independent motors that all turn at the same speed; especially, picture and sound running synchronously on separate machines.

Internegative: Low-contrast film negative made from positive film.

Interpositive: A low-contrast color positive made from an original film negative.

Jingle: A musical composition associated with a specific product or service.

Key frame: The one frame in a sequence or complete commercial that best represents the "look" of the final production.

Key light: The main source of directional light on a scene.

Key numbers: Edge numbers placed on negative film at one-foot intervals; these numbers print through so that print and negative can be matched.

Kick light: A small light used to accent an object or person, usually from the side or rear.

Kinescope: A motion-picture record of a television image; a rather primitive tape-to-film transfer.

Laboratory: The organization that processes and prints all the film elements in a motion picture.

Latent image: The image on an exposed piece of film before it is developed.

Legal clearance: Opinions from lawyers as to a commercial's being broadcast without legal problems.

Limbo: A location without any specific identity, used as a background.

Limiting resolution: The 525 lines per picture height used in standard television broadcasting and recording.

Lip sync: Precise match between lip movement and speech sounds.

Liquid head: A tripod head in which the bearing surface consists of a liquid film.

Logo: The customer's identifying trademark or design.

Log sheet: A form kept by crew members that accurately logs all shots with remarks and instructions.

Loop: A piece of film that is spliced head to tail so it runs continuously. Used to postdub sound and to repeat background action.

Low key: Lighting that has a predominance of dark tones with a large amount of detailed shadow areas.

Magazine: The part of the motion-picture camera that contains the film. Professional cameras have separate magazines that are attached to the camera.

Markup: The percentage added to cost to allow for overhead and profit.

Master: The main recording from which duplicates are made.

Match dissolve: An optical effect in which one element perfectly matches another as the scene slowly changes.

Matte: High-contrast film that is used to block out light and permit exposure of motion picture film on an optical bench. Also, a mask determining the area of the image exposed on motion-picture film in a camera or printer.

Mixer: The chief audio engineer for original sound recordings or final mixes of previously recorded material.

Monitor: Any television set, but usually a closed-circuit set that shows a high-quality picture; used for program checking.

Moviola: Manufacturer of editing equipment; also, a motion-picture editing machine.

NABET: National Association of Broadcast Employees and Technicians, a union of workers in the broadcast industry.

NBC: National Broadcasting Company, a national television network.

NG take: An unacceptable (no good) recorded scene.

Noise: An undesired sound on a recording or, on videotape, the poor quality of the picture because of overamplification of the video signal; the equivalent of grain in film.

Off line: Not suitable for broadcast.

One-light print: A rough, untimed print made with one exposure light setting on the printer.

O & O stations: Stations that are owned and operated by networks.

Optical bench: A critically controlled series of cameras and projectors used to combine images in selective recopying for special visuals.

Optical effect: A special visual that cannot be realized with traditional photography. It is usually a combination of many special visuals combined on an optical bench, and includes wipes, flips, freeze frames, and matte shots.

Optical sound: Photographic sound recording used on sound-on-film (SOF) prints.

Oscilloscope: A wave-form monitor used by video technicians to check signals and analyze picture quality.

Oxide: The metalic medium applied to tape in which particles are rearranged to form an electrical signal.

Pencil test: A test of the pencil sketches that will be used for final animation.

Perforation: The holes along the sides of film that are used for transporting it through camera, projectors, and printers. etc.

Pickup tube: Small tube in a camera on which the image is focused.

Pixillation: Quick motion, used to describe stop motion with live people.

Playback: Playing recorded sound through a speaker system for review or for use as a reference during shooting.

Pool: A group of commercials produced at the same time.

Prime time: Three consecutive hours of television time between 6:00 P.M. and 10:00 P.M.

Processing: The laboratory procedures of developing, printing, washing, and drying sensitized film.

Producer: An advertising-agency term for the person responsible for TV-commercial production. The production studio also has a producer (or production manager), as do large advertisers.

Producer/director: A production company classification indicating an individual who not only handles the production of a commercial but also directs it.

Product strategy: The merchandising of a product, usually the result of research.

Production insurance: The many types of insurance needed include negative insurance, weather insurance, high-risk, and personnel.

Projector: A machine that projects an image, usually motion pictures or slides.

Props: Properties that are used on the set or are necessary in any other part of production. Small props that can be easily handled are called hand props.

Push: A technique whereby film is over-developed to increase density or videotape is overamplified to increase brightness. Generally used to record in low-light situations.

Quadraplex recorder (quad): A two-inch videotape recorder with four record and play-back picture heads.

Random access: The ability of a viewing machine to recall material independent of its loca-ation or sequence.

Real time: A function that takes place at the same time that it is demanded (actual time).

Redress: To change properties on a set or on location.

Reduction print: A film print made from a nega-tive with a larger gauge than the print; generally, a 16-mm print made from a 35-mm negative.

Reference print: An approved print that is re-tained to check the quality of release prints.

Release prints: Final quantity prints that are ready to be screened.

Rerecording: Combining several sound tracks onto a single track by mixing them together.

Reuse payment: Residuals; payments to per-formers for broadcast uses of a commercial.

Reversal film: Film that is exposed and spe-cially developed into a positive rather than a negative.

Residual: Payments made after the perfor-mance fee, usually to a performer during the run of a commercial.

Rigging: Construction of equipment or gear to assist in shooting a scene; everything from sets to camera positions, from safety equipment to stunts.

Ripple dissolve: An optical effect of a dissolve buried in a wavy or swimming look, frequently used to start a dream sequence.

Roll: A lack of vertical synchronization, causing the picture to move up and down.

Rough cut: Early version of a commercial with-out opticals and before final approval.

Running shot: Photography with camera and subject both moving swiftly, as a moving car photographed from a camera car.

Rushes: Overnight prints from newly exposed and developed negatives; dailies, work print.

SAG: Screen Actors Guild, a union that repre-sents performers working in film.

Safe area: The area of a television picture that always appears on home receivers; of special concern for type and logos.

Satellite: An orbiting space station that can re-lay television signals from their origination point to any point in the world; used for distributing TV commercials quickly.

Scale: The minimum rate of pay in a classifica-tion of employment, established by a union for its members.

Scan line: An individual line of a television pic-ture; one of the 525 lines that make up the standard picture. Each line is formed by the rapid movement of an electronic beam.

Scanning: The electronic construction of a tele-vision picture. An electronic gun sweeps across the picture 525 times in 1/30 of a second.

Scratch print: Stock footage sent for review; it is scratched to prevent use without payment.

Scratch track: Rough sound track used as edi-tor's guideline.

Script clerk: The person who notes details and timings of each take for postproduction.

SEG: Screen Extras Guild, a union that repre-sents nonfeature performers.

Segue: A change from one music to another without a noticeable shift; also used to describe a soft visual move from one image to another.

Shading: Adjusting the contrast and brightness within the television picture during the broad-cast or recording.

Shooting script: Final script approved for pro-duction. Scenes are usually timed for length and accompanied by a storyboard.

Shotgun microphone: An extremely unidi-rectional microphone.

Signal: Picture or sound information trans-posed into electric impulses.

Signatory: A company that signs an agreement with a union or guild to abide by its working conditions and pay scales.

Skip printing: An optical procedure in which only some frames on the original negative, se-lected at regular intervals, are printed; projec-tion results in speeded-up action.

Slate: An identification recorded on film or videotape; on film, the familiar clap board is photographed.

Slides: 35-mm double-frame transparencies mounted in two-by-two-inch mounts, frequently used for superimpositions, dealer commercials, local spots, and station identification.

Slit scan: The streaking effect of animation produced by computer-controlled animation stands.

Slow motion: Shooting motion pictures at a faster rate of frames per second than standard projection, thus slowing down action when projected.

SMPTE: Society of Motion Picture and Television Engineers, a professional organization that initiates practices and standards within the industry.

Snorkel: A periscope lens attachment that permits a camera viewpoint not possible with the standard lens position.

Sound advance: The number of frames that the sound is ahead of the picture on a composite print. This is necessary because the projector's sound pickup is twenty-six frames ahead of the picture. Videotape has no sound advance.

Sound on film (SOF): A composite print including both picture and sound.

Sound speed: The standard speed for sound motion pictures, twenty-four frames per second in projection.

Spider box: Electrical junction box used on stage and location.

Split screen: A screen divided into sections with separate pictures in each section. On film this effect is produced on an optical bench; on videotape it is made electronically with an effects generator.

Sponsor: The advertiser who purchases air time for an advertising message on a television program.

Spot: A type of light that projects a spot effect. It also denotes a television commercial, because each occupies a small time segment.

Spot time buy: Purchasing air time on a station-by-station basis.

Star filter: A cross-hatched filter that makes every highlight look like a star.

Station break: A brief break in programming for a station identification.

Steadicam: A camera mount suspended and balanced on the cameraman to reduce jerky movements.

Step printer: A motion-picture printing machine with intermittent action that prints one frame at a time; an optical printer.

Stock: Material in a library; footage, music, and still photos can be obtained from stock.

Stop motion: A visual technique in which the appearance of motion is achieved by shooting one frame at a time and moving the object slightly between exposures. In projection, the object moves.

Storyboard: An artist's representation of a finished commercial. Drawings of key frames of each scene are accompanied by the related portion of the script.

Stylist: A crew member concerned with the procuring of wardrobe and props; works with art director.

Sweep: A set that has no horizon line and sweeps from floor to wall. Also, an electronic video scan.

Switcher: An electronic control panel that can change inputs and outputs on demand. It can select a picture from two or more sources.

Sync generator: A unit that emits exact pulses to control TV picture scanning and brightness.

Synchronizer: A device used in editing for maintaining exact sync between two or more pieces of film.

Take: Scene or part of a scene photographed without interruption.

Talent: Generally, on-camera performers.

Tape: The general term for nonperforated ribbon of magnetic material on which sound and pictures are recorded.

Target audience: The special group (age, ethnic, income level, and occupation) of viewers at which a commercial's sales pitch is aimed.

TBC (Time Base Corrector): A black box unit designed to compensate for errors introduced into video signals on videotape. This unit makes it possible to play videotape without problems.

Teleprompter: A mechanical or electronic device used to prompt actors. The script is enlarged and can be read from the performer's position. It can be placed off camera or directly over the lens, using mirrors.

Testing: Showing a proposed advertising campaign to a sample audience.

Test spot: A commercial made for testing a concept or product.

Time buys: Broadcast time purchased by an advertising agency for its client.

Time code: Videotape code using time as a locating system. The code includes hours, minutes, seconds, and frames; it is recorded on the tape and appears on a monitor.

Track: Portion of film print or videotape containing sound. Also, the metal guides a dolly rolls on.

Traffic: The handling of finished elements between an advertising agency and the media.

UHF: Ultra-high frequency, television channels 14 to 83.

VCR: Videotape cassette recorder, a tape recorder that uses ¾-inch or ½-inch tape.

VHF: Very-high frequency, television channels 2 to 13.

Video assist: A small video pickup designed to be fitted to the eyepiece of a film camera. It allows bystanders to view the picture being photographed from the camera viewpoint while it records.

Video camera chain: The basic machines of a videotaping session: TV camera, power supply, amplifier, camera control unit, and recorder.

Video disc: A record that stores video signals.

Videotape: The magnetic recording material used for recording pictures and sound.

Voice actor: An off-camera character voice.

Voice-over: Off-screen narration.

VTR: Videotape recording, the reel-to-reel method of recording with two-inch or one-inch tape.

Weather day: An allowance in a production estimate for additional payment if poor weather is encountered.

Wild: Said of sound that is made independently of the camera operation.

Wipe: An optical effect of one picture wiping off another.

Work print: A print from the original camera negative that is used for editing; also called dailies and rushes.

Zoom lens: A lens with a focal length that can change.

INDEX